The Unnamed Devotional

Lisa Buffaloe

The Unnamed Devotional

© 2016 Lisa Buffaloe (Updated 070723)
Published by John 15:11 Publications
Visit the author's website at http://lisabuffaloe.com

Scripture taken from the New Century Version® (NCV). Copyright © 2005 by Thomas Nelson, Inc. Used by permission. All rights reserved.

Living Bible (TLB) The Living Bible copyright © 1971 by Tyndale House Foundation. Used by permission of Tyndale House Publishers Inc., Carol Stream, Illinois 60188. All rights reserved.

Scripture taken from the NEW AMERICAN STANDARD BIBLE® (NASB), Copyright © 1960, 1962, 1963 ,1968, 1971, 1972, 1973 ,1975, 1977, 1995 by The Lockman Foundation. Used by permission.

Scripture quotations marked (NLT) are taken from the Holy Bible, New Living Translation, copyright © 1996, 2004, 2007 by Tyndale House Foundation. Used by permission of Tyndale House Publishers, Inc., Carol Stream, Illinois 60188. All rights reserved.

THE HOLY BIBLE, NEW INTERNATIONAL VERSION®, NIV® Copyright © 1973, 1978, 1984, 2011 by Biblica, Inc.™ Used by permission. All rights reserved worldwide.

Scripture taken from the New King James Version®. Copyright © 1982 by Thomas Nelson, Inc. Used by permission. All rights reserved.

Scripture taken from *The Message*. Copyright © 1993, 1994, 1995, 1996, 2000, 2001, 2002. Used by permission of NavPress Publishing Group.

Scripture quotations marked HCSB are taken from the Holman Christian Standard Bible®, Copyright © 1999, 2000, 2002, 2003, 2009 by Holman Bible Publishers. Used by permission. Holman Christian Standard Bible®, Holman CSB®, and HCSB® are federally registered trademarks of Holman Bible Publishers. Scripture marked ERV, Copyright ©2006 World Bible Translation Center.

Cover design: Lisa Buffaloe

ASIN: B01FQ8RNNM
ISBN-10 : 0692691367
ISBN-13 : 978-0692691366

~ *Dedication and Thanks* ~

To my amazing God and Savior, Jesus Christ. I'm eternally grateful for Your grace, mercy, and unfailing love. Thank You for Your rescue and restoration and for the blessing of writing about You. I can never do enough to thank You.

Thank you also to my sweet husband and son, thank you for your constant encouragement and love. I love you both.

Unnamed

Unnamed – without a name; nameless. Not indicated or mentioned by name; unidentified, unknown.

I worked on the book for months and never could come up with a name other than The Unnamed Devotional. Then I realized so many people feel lost in a sea of humanity, just another unknown face in the crowd.

We all have our stories of feeling nameless.

An author traveled to Zimbabwe and said orphaned children clutched at them and called out their own names. They wanted food, but more than that, they wanted someone to know they existed.

We all want to know someone knows we exist. The world can be such a lonely place. Many times, I've felt no one noticed me or cared to even know my name. Thirty-five moves presented numerous opportunities to be the unknown outcast.

I want you to know, no matter how alone you feel and how unnoticed, God knows your name. He loves you. He knew you before you were even born. He knit you together in your mother's womb and knows you so intimately he knows the number of hairs on your head. You are so very known and so very loved.

I love you with an everlasting love. Before I formed you in the womb, I knew you. I created your inmost being, knit you together in your mother's womb, I will help you. Even the hairs of your head are numbered, and I will be with you always (Jeremiah 31:3, Jeremiah 1:5, Psalm 139:13, Isaiah 44:2, Matthew 10:30, Matthew 28:20).

Clark Kent or Superman?

God calls the most unlikely people to follow Him, often choosing the ones who aren't the smartest, strongest, or richest.

God chooses the Clark Kents instead of the Supermen, and then turns the Clark Kents into Supermen.

Gideon was the youngest from the "least" tribe and yet God turned him into a warrior and deliverer.

David was a lowly shepherd turned into giant-slayer and king.

Fishermen became fishers of men and turned the world upside down.

God's view is opposite of the worldview. With God, the least becomes the greatest, and the last becomes the first.

Jesus sacrificed His life to give new life to all who believe, and Christians exchange their lives to become new creations—sons and daughters of The King of kings.

You aren't what others have said about you, you aren't a label, your true identity is God's child. As His child, you have the power of God within you to change you into what He created you to be. For nothing is impossible for God.

Are you staying a Clark Kent, or will you embrace your true identity and live in God's power?

As for me? I want to fly! Join me? Let's fly!

"But God has chosen the foolish things of the world to shame the wise, and God has chosen the weak things of the world to shame the things which are strong, and the base things of the world and the despised God has chosen, the things that are not, so that He may nullify the things that are. Now to Him who is able to do far more abundantly beyond all that we ask or think, according to the power that works within us, to Him be the glory in the church and in Christ Jesus to all generations forever and ever. Amen." ~ 1 Corinthians 1:27-28 (NASB), Ephesians 3:20-21 (NASB)

Awe-inspiring, Jaw-dropping Equipped

Throughout the Bible God blesses His children with awe-inspiring, jaw-dropping power and creativity. The story of Bazelel fascinates me. Who was he and why was he hand-picked by God? Chapter after chapter in Exodus tells what Bazelel crafted and created. Wow, wow, wow!

"Moses then said to the Israelites: 'Look, the Lord has appointed by name Bezalel son of Uri, son of Hur, of the tribe of Judah. He has filled him with God's Spirit, with wisdom, understanding, and ability in every kind of craft to design artistic works in gold, silver, and bronze, to cut gemstones for mounting, and to carve wood for work in every kind of artistic craft. He has also given both him and Oholiab son of Ahisamach, of the tribe of Dan, the ability to teach others." ~ Exodus 35:30-34 (NASB)

What Bazelel accomplished was amazing because of our amazing God. "...The Lord has given them wisdom and understanding to know how to do all the work..." ~ Exodus 36:1 (NASB)

When God wants a job done, He can do it Himself, but so very often He chooses someone for an assignment. Whatever God calls us to do, He will be the One who gives us the wisdom and power to accomplish that task. God does exceedingly, superabundantly more than we could ask or think (Ephesians 3:20).

The original Greek definition for equipping is SO much bigger and even more exciting than I imagined. According to Strong's G2675 – katartizō (Equipping or perfecting) means to render, to mend, to repair, to complete, put in order, arrange, adjust, prepare, ethically: to strengthen, perfect, complete, make one what he ought to be, frame, restore, make perfect.

Wow! Isn't that cool? God's equipping is multi-functional, on-going, constantly adjusting, refitting, repairing, mending, setting right, restoring, to make us perfectly fitted for His assignments. Now that's some awesome equipping!

And the more we read God's word, the more we are further equipped because "all Scripture is inspired by God and profitable for teaching, for reproof, for correction, for training in righteousness; so that the man of God may be adequate, equipped for every good work." ~ 2 Timothy 3:16-17 (NASB)

God's gifts come to us all. "And He gave some as apostles, and some as prophets, and some as evangelists, and some as pastors and teachers, for the equipping of the saints for the work of service, to the building up of the body of Christ" ~ Ephesians 4:11-12 (NASB)

Another amazing fact, "it is God who is at work in you, both to will and to work for His good pleasure." ~ Philippians 2:13 (NASB)

You aren't just equipped, you are super-abundantly, powerfully, exceedingly more than you can ask or imagine, awe-inspiring, jaw-dropping equipped through the MIGHTY power of Christ!

Unfailing

The worries of coordinating an upcoming move with movers, car shipping, packing items in the bedrooms, office, bathrooms, garage, finding flights, and working with people in another state for when we would arrive, had me tossing and turning in the night. I prayed for God's mercy, prayed for help, and apologized to God I was worried and wasn't resting.

Since I was having a hard time, I tried to refocus my focus by turning my prayers into praises that God is bigger than my worries, bigger than the moving issues, and bigger than my fears.

Then the still small voice asked, "Have I ever failed you?"

Tears flowed as I realized God has never failed me. Yes, I've been through hard times and difficult problems, but God has never failed me and will never fail me. He is always there for whatever we go through.

God's love is unfailing. He is unfailing. God won't ever fail you.

For those who are alone (even in a marriage), single, divorced, or widowed, God is an unfailing husband, an unfailing Father to the fatherless, and an unfailing defender of widows and orphans.

Life contains hardships and difficulties. People fail us because they are imperfect humans. Would you take a moment to read the following verses and apply them to your life and make them personal?

"For your husband is your Maker, whose name is the Lord of hosts; and your Redeemer is the Holy One of Israel, who is called the God of all the earth." ~ Isaiah 54:5 (NASB)

"If my father and mother leave me, the Lord will take me in." ~ Psalm 27:10 (NCV)

"He helps orphans and widows, and He loves foreigners and gives them food and clothes." ~ Deuteronomy 10:18 (NCV)

"A father of the fatherless and a judge for the widows, is God in His holy habitation." ~ Psalm 68:5 (NASB)

"The Lord appeared to us in the past, saying: 'I have loved you with an everlasting love; I have drawn you with unfailing kindness." ~ Jeremiah 31:3 (NIV)

No matter who you are, hard times may come, difficulties may arise, but God will not fail you and always loves you!

Call Your Father

We once had a very cool, very smart cat named Roosevelt Franklin. When he became injured in a fight, he would walk down the street and meow at the neighbor's house. The neighbor just happened to be a veterinarian. I'm not sure we ever received a bill for Roosevelt's care.

Roosevelt would even take on dogs who dared to venture into our yard. The cat would sit sphinxlike and wait. The dogs would bark, run around him, and try to egg him into a fight. But Roosevelt? He'd just sit there ... until the dog got too close. Then the big cat would rise up on his back paws, grab the canine by the shoulders, and flip the surprised animal on his back. Those dogs would run off yelping, and Roosevelt would saunter away with a satisfied expression on his cat-face.

When we moved to the country, we heard Roosevelt's muffled meow coming from behind the house. With a bounce in his step and a smile on his kitty face, he presented us with his latest catch – a snake.

Problem was, he had caught the snake by the tail. And now the serpent had curled around the cat's face and protruded from Roosevelt's forehead like a Cleopatra headdress.

Both the cat and snake seemed pleased with the arrangement, until Roosevelt opened his mouth to tell us further about his adventure. The snake took the opportunity to run. A loose snake is not a good thing, so my mighty, snake-hunting father came to the rescue.

Roosevelt had the right idea, but his execution was flawed. We also need to remember not to toy with an enemy. Satan is out to steal, kill, and destroy. He is the father of all lies. The devil accuses, condemns, and is always looking for someone to devour. He manipulates, twists around minds and twists God's truth.

Trying to combat the enemy in our own power is like Roosevelt with the snake by the tail. The cat thought he was the conqueror, but the snake wasn't the least bit flustered.

No matter how tough you are, or how cool you are, you need your Heavenly Father when combating the enemy. Nothing, and no enemy, is too big for our all-powerful Father God.

When you are in a battle with the enemy, call your Father!

"I call upon the Lord, who is worthy to be praised, and I am saved from my enemies." ~ Psalm 18:3 (NASB)

"Who will separate us from the love of Christ? Will tribulation, or distress, or persecution, or famine, or nakedness, or peril, or sword? ...in all these things we overwhelmingly conquer through Him who loved us." ~ Romans 8:35, 37 (NASB

"Turn to Me and be saved, all the ends of the earth; for I am God, and there is no other." ~ Isaiah 45:22 (NASB)

When did it start?

Where did it start?
When did you stop living?
When did the fire grow cold?
How did the passion die?

Disappointment, heartache, loss, tragedy, and trials take their toll. Sometimes it all seems too much, too much pain and sorrow, and the heart withers and crawls behind the ribcage of a wounded soul.

When did your heart start to hide? When did it all become too much to move forward? Where is your stuck place, your stopping point? Do you know?

My walking wounded friend, I want you to know your heart can be soothed in the comforting love of God.

Please know and remember your Heavenly Father loves you and cares for you.

I want you to know God will never forsake you even when it seems all have forsaken you.

I need you to know in a world full of trouble, life can be overcome with the One who is The Overcomer.

You need the gentle touch of grace.

In your loss, you need to know your loved one is safe in God's arms.

In your need, you need to know God provides in amazing ways.

In your weakness, you need to know God's strength remains.

Please talk to God. Please ask Him to reveal the lies the enemy has planted in your wounds. Please ask God to show you His truth.

Where did it start? Go back with God, go back with His truth. For in the truth of God, a stopping place becomes the start of restoration, healing, renewal, and a new life.

Would you be willing to pray with me?

Heavenly Father, show me where the enemy has planted lies in my wounds. Reveal the evil ways the enemy has twisted what happened to me and my loved ones. Show me the truth of the situation and the truth of what You do with every situation. Show me the good. Show me the next steps. Show me how to move forward. Shower me with Your healing, restoring grace. Shower me with Your life that brings life. Restart and unwither my withered heart and restore me with Your unfailing love.

Please apply God's truth, where does your help come from? Your help comes from the Lord, the maker of heaven and earth. He heals the brokenhearted and saves those whose spirits have been crushed. Every one of your tears He gently places in His bottle. God's compassions never fail. You are safe and sheltered in God's unfailing love. He loves you with an everlasting love. Every day in Christ, a new beginning has begun. And one day when you are safe in God's arms in heaven, He will wipe away every tear and there will be no more mourning or sorrow or pain (Psalm 121:1-2, Psalm 147:3, Psalm 34:18, Psalm 56:8, Lamentations 3:22-23, Psalm 36:5-7, Jeremiah 31:3, 2 Corinthians 5:17, Revelation 21:4).

Take it Back!

God has been working (in me and with me) to help me understand some of His truths. Satan can't rob a Christian of their salvation, but the enemy wants us to be hopeless, defeated, and ineffective in God's kingdom. God gives us freedom, and with God's help we can take back what the enemy has stolen from us.

The Israelites had a choice in taking possession of the land God had given them, "How long will you delay going out to take possession of the land the Lord... gave you?" (Joshua 18:3)

I realized I also have choices.

Several months ago, I had a very troubling dream. Although half of the dream was positive for our son, for me I was literally left in the dark. I couldn't see the future, couldn't see anything. I was sitting in blackness. I had another negative dream, and when I prayed, I sensed the Lord telling me I didn't have to stay there.

Oh.

I didn't have to sit and stew and analyze, and I didn't have to stay in the bad situation where the dream had left me. I could just walk out. I could visualize the dream ending in a different manner. Wow, how cool is that!

Unfortunately, I walked out of one dream but still sat in the darkness in the other. Why, I don't know. Sigh...

When I talked about the situation with a friend God's truth became clear. There is no darkness in God. Jesus is the light of the world and Jesus lives in me, so I always have the light of Christ. His Word is a lamp to my feet and light for my path. I didn't have to sit in darkness! I ripped back the curtain on that dream and stepped into the light.

What the enemy had stolen, I took back!

Then the other day my computer started scrolling through beautiful outdoor pictures of a previous place where we had lived. Unfortunately, they reminded me of a negative situation, and I turned away. In the quiet of my soul I felt a gentle reminder the Lord had made the beauty of that place for me to enjoy.

In turning away, I was turning away from His blessing. In response, I once again enjoyed my photos. I took back what the enemy had stolen from me.

When the wives and children of David and his army were captured, David and his forces went and took them back by force (see 1 Samuel 30).

Take it back! With God's power, take back what the enemy has stolen from you. Take back your joy. Take back the good memories. Turn the bad dreams into a good ending. We have been given (gifted) this life, but we must take possession. Drive out the enemy. No enemy, no stronghold, is too big for God. Drive out fear, worry, greed, lust, unforgiveness, idolatry... with the truth of God's Word and who you are in Christ.

What the enemy has stolen, go through Christ and take it back! Take back your past. Give it to God and let Him take it back. Let His Grace and love wash it away and let Him take away the ugly and replace it with His restoration.

Don't make the temporary, the permanent. Stop the blame game and walk in God's freedom. God is bigger than your pain, your past, your sin, your shame, anything you've been through.

It is freedom Christ set you free. Wherever there is darkness, let the light of Christ shine and take back what the enemy has stolen.

Freedom isn't just for the strong or a certain type of person, it's for anyone who is in Christ Jesus. He is freedom. Whatever is hindering you from walking free in the Lord, take it back with God's truth!

"The people who walk in darkness will see a great light; those who live in a dark land, **the light will shine on them.**" ~ Isaiah 9:2 (NASB)

"For You light my lamp; **The Lord my God illumines my darkness.**" ~ Psalm 18:28 (NASB)

"With the arrival of Jesus, the Messiah, that fateful dilemma is resolved. Those who enter into Christ's being-here-for-us no longer have to live under a continuous, low-lying black cloud. A new power is in operation. **The Spirit of life in Christ, like a strong wind, has magnificently cleared the air, freeing you** from a fated lifetime of brutal tyranny at the hands of sin and death." ~ Romans 8:1-2 (MSG)

"If I take the wings of the dawn, if I dwell in the remotest part of the sea, even there **Your hand will lead me, and Your right hand will lay hold of me**. If I say, 'Surely the darkness will overwhelm me, and the light around me will be night, **even the darkness is not dark to You, and the night is as bright as the day**. Darkness and light are alike to You. For You formed my inward parts; You wove me in my mother's womb. I will give thanks to You, for I am fearfully and wonderfully made; wonderful are Your works, and my soul knows it very well." ~ Psalm 139:9-14 (NASB)

(Emphasis added on scripture).

Will The Battle

Are you in a spiritual battle? When problems are coming from something other than health-related issues. When nothing seems to work. When life is a roller coaster ride with hair-raising drops and upside-down turns and even the barf-bags can't be found, those are the times that it's a battle of the will—a battle to will yourself to remember how battles are won.

It's willing ourselves to remember the truth of who we are in Christ and are eternally safe and invincible in Christ.

It's willing ourselves to remember God promised to fight for us. He promised to never leave us or forsake us. He promised His love is unfailing.

It's willing ourselves to remember battles aren't won by caving into the enemy. Battles are won by remembering as a Christian we are on the winning team.

It's willing ourselves to remember crawling off the battlefield isn't an option because until the end a battle will always rage. Crawling leaves us defenseless, but standing firm gives us firm-footing in Christ our Solid Rock. And even when you can only crawl, your soul can always stand!

It's willing ourselves to remember the enemy may battle, but the final war has already been won.

It's willing ourselves to remember we are to run into the battles where God calls us because no battle is too big for our God.

Satan wants us to withdraw, to put down our swords, to curl into a ball, and have nothing to do with anyone or with God.

The enemy wants to silence you, get you off the battlefield so your testimony can't help and encourage others. Your life is here to point others to The Life, so don't believe for a moment you don't have a purpose.

Wherever you are in the battle, remember you are never alone. Watch for how God is working, how God is using you, and has positioned you to help others.

Let's keep the enemy from winning any more ground! Let's stop believing the lie we should crawl off the battlefield.

Beyond human sight, the battles rage between the forces of good and evil. The enemy is slinking around, sliming his slime in our thoughts and trying every dirty trick to keep people away from the love of God.

Satan wants Christians to be ineffective or throw in the towel. Our hearts are under attack because the enemy wants our hearts to stop beating passionately for Christ. Don't let the enemy win! Put up heart guards by listening to God's word and keeping the wisdom learned in God's truth (Proverbs 4:20-23).

If you feel surrounded by the enemy, don't worry, that only makes them easier to hit.

When fear attacks, attack fear with God's truth and watch fear turn tail and run. The Bible is an offensive weapon against the enemy providing the sword of truth, and that sword slashes away every attack of the enemy.

Read God's word, say the words, go to God with every request because God is more than a safe place to run, God is our defender and protector. He is our shield.

"The Lord is my rock, my protection, my Savior. My God is my rock. I can run to him for safety. He is my shield and my saving strength, my defender." ~ Psalm 18:2 (NCV)

God will NEVER leave you or forsake you. God is GREATER than anyone or anything and nothing is impossible for God. We may be battling, but we know the final battle is already won!

If you are in Christ, you are on the winning team. Stand firm, stand strong, raise your sword of the Spirit and remember you are a child of the King!

The Blessing Game

Have you ever been blessed? Perhaps someone gave you an unexpected gift or sent a message at just the right time. Blessings bring encouragement. Blessings help us know we are noticed and sometimes can even a save a life. Blessings matter!

After being inspired by watching a video where a man paid for people's groceries. He would pay, tell them God is good, and walk away. The recipient would be left stunned at the kindness of a stranger. The impact on their lives was obvious and beautiful. I wanted to join in the beauty of that blessing, to encourage someone, lift their spirits, and tell them they are loved by God.

I posted a blessing game on my website asking if my readers would prayerfully consider joining me in the blessing game. I asked them to take a moment to send someone a blessing by sending a note, or calling, or helping someone in need.

Sadly, it seemed very few noticed. I even gave away a $25.00 Amazon gift card. I tried to bless, but not many would enter, and it made me so sad. Then I thought of how God blesses us and yet so very few notice His blessings.

Every single moment of every single day, God holds out the blessings of an amazing sunrise. God blesses with beating hearts and breath for each day. God blesses with provision and blesses and blesses and blesses and blesses. Because of God's nature, because He is love, He keeps sending blessings EVERY. Single Moment. Of EVERY single day.

As God blesses, will you bless others because God has blessed you? Who can you bless?

"Here is a simple rule of thumb for behavior: Ask yourself what you want people to do for you; then grab the initiative and do it for them! If you only love the lovable, do you expect a pat on the back? Run-of-the-mill sinners do that. If you only help those who help you, do you expect a medal? Garden-variety sinners do that.

"If you only give for what you hope to get out of it, do you think that's charity? The stingiest of pawnbrokers does that. I tell you, love your enemies. Help and give without expecting a return. You'll never—I promise—regret it. Live out this God-created identity the way our Father lives toward us, generously and graciously, even when we're at our worst. Our Father is kind; you be kind." ~ Luke 6:31-36 (MSG)

Blah

Have you ever had those blah days, weeks, months, years... where life seemed joyless? I'm not a fan of blah.

Blah is defined by the dictionary as "a feeling of boredom, lethargy, or general dissatisfaction."

Ugh. Blah is so blah and bland. Blah sucks away life and joy. There are times blah makes me anxious because I don't like being blah. The blah just becomes too much, and I'll sit and mope about being blah. Unfortunately, that only leads to more blah.

I can ponder the blahs all day, lay awake in the night and stare at my blahs, but I don't want the blahs. I don't want to live in a state of blah. Blah does not have state rights! So, I'm thinking I need to do some blah banning.

Even the Psalmist had a case of the blahs, but he found a cure. "Why are you cast down, O my soul? And why are you disquieted within me? Hope in God, for I shall yet praise Him for the help of His countenance. ~ Psalm 42:5 (NKJV)

So, let's
Banish
Lethargy
And
Hope in God!

When our focus is returned to God and praising God, the blahs are driven away. The truth of God and His promises, His facts, are the cure for the blah ailment.

If I'm blah because I don't think things are going to work out, I can look to the truth of Romans 8:28 "And we know that all things work together for good to those who love God, to those who are the called according to His purpose." ~ Romans 8:28 (NKJV)

If I'm blah because the energy is low, I can look to the truth that God "gives power to the weak, and to those who have no might He increases strength." ~ Isaiah 40:29 (NKJV)

If I'm blah because I wonder if my pitiful prayers are being heard, I can look to the truth "the Spirit also helps in our weaknesses. For we do not know what we should pray for as we ought, but the Spirit Himself makes intercession for us with groanings which cannot be uttered." ~ Romans 8:26 (NKJV)

When I'm blah because this world just seems to have too much trouble, I can look to what Jesus promised in John 16:33 "in Me you may have peace. In the world you will have tribulation; but be of good cheer, I have overcome the world." ~ John 16:33 (NKJV)

Even on the blahest days, we can find the hope needed to banish the blahs with the truth of God's word!

Unboxed

I keep thinking I need to act in a certain way because I'm a Christian, and as a result I box myself into an imaginary box.

My self-made confinement never fits because we are not boxed-in or created to look like clones of one another, we are to allow Christ to mold us into His image. His image is unique, beautiful, fluid and never confined or molded to man's ideals or man's image.

Oh, my goodness, I have limited myself for years worried about everything I say and do, and goodness knows makeup must be worn if stepping outside the door. I feel guilty if I don't have a quiet time, then feel guilty if my quiet time isn't long enough, or if I spend too much time doing one thing and not another thing. Guilt boxes me in until I can't move or breathe, and I lose my joy. Gasp, wheeze...

I realized perhaps on every new day that God just wants me to open my eyes and tell Him good morning and that I love Him. I think God wants us to crawl out of self-made boxes, or boxes that someone else has placed around us, and enjoy Him.

I'm the one who has made being a Christian SO hard. When I release all my worries about being "good" enough and acting "good" enough, I remember the simplicity of the life God has called us to live. "...the Lord has told you what is good, and this is what he requires of you: to do what is right, to love mercy, and to walk humbly with your God." ~ Micah 6:8 (NLT)

Jesus said the greatest commandment is, "'love the Lord your God with all your heart, all your soul, and all your mind." ~ Matthew 22:37 (NLT) I can love God freely instead of thinking I need to do something to check a mark on a list or please people.

Therefore, when the guilt thing is guilting me into feeling miserable, I need to remember condemnation doesn't come from God. It was for freedom Christ set us free. In Christ we are free to be His unique creations, walking with Him, loving Him and loving others, unboxed to walk in the newness of Him.

So, if you are feeling boxed in, join me by jumping out of the box and embracing who you are in Christ!

"Christ has set us free to live a free life. So, take your stand! Never again let anyone put a harness of slavery on you." ~ Galatians 5:1 (MSG) (Or a box around you!)

Getting Well

Within the book of John, we find a story about a man who had been an invalid for thirty-eight years. He and many others, the blind, lame and paralyzed laid waiting by the pool of Bethesda.

The Bethesda pool was no ordinary pool. People believed the water would occasionally be stirred by the touch of an angel and the first one in would be healed. Day after day those needing a miracle watched and waited.

Then Jesus stood next to a man. "When Jesus saw him lying there, and knew that he had already been a long time in that condition, He said to him, 'Do you wish to get well?'" ~ John 5:6 (NASB)

The man at the pool was in the masses, yet all alone. Did family and friends take him there when the illness first struck, or had they cared for a time and then lost hope?

Jesus didn't address everyone. He addressed this man. I find it interesting Jesus asked him such a question. The man had been an invalid for thirty-eight years; wouldn't he *want* to be well? I think I would have said YES! I would have begged and pleaded for any help offered.

However, "The sick man answered Him, 'Sir, I have no man to put me into the pool when the water is stirred up; but while I am coming, another steps down before me.'" John 5:7 (NKJV)

The man focused on his own weakness and own inabilities, perhaps he was even comfortable with his uncomfortable life. Resigned to his fate, that no one was there to help him, the man never answered Jesus' question.

The man answered out of his lack.

Jesus answered with unmerited grace.

"Jesus said to him, 'Rise, take up your bed and walk.'" ~ John 5:8 (NKJV)

When Jesus walked into the man's life, he was given the option to get well. The choice was his.

The man couldn't heal himself, but he could respond to the words Jesus spoke. "And immediately the man was made well, took up his bed, and walked." ~ John 5:8-9 (NKJV)

Life is hard. Bad things happen to us and those we love. The past can cling to us like a devastating illness. We cannot always choose what happened to us or what is happening in our lives, but we do have an option how we respond.

If we refuse to release our pain, infirmities, aching memories, or wrongs committed against us, we become like the invalid at the pool complaining no one is ever there to carry us, even as the Great Physician stands with His hand outstretched asking "Do you want to get well?"

Freedom and healing will not come until what we are carrying or suffering is given to God -- completely and totally. Jesus asks, "Do you want to get well?"

The enemy wants you to stay down, in the midst of your past, stay in your unforgiveness, yet Jesus says, "Rise and walk."

If we believe Jesus Christ took on our sins, was raised from the dead, and offers eternal life, why the hesitation to believe God can heal us from our past?

Man says some things are just too difficult to overcome. God says nothing is impossible.

Man says there is no hope for restoration, yet God is The God of restorations.

Man says there is nothing good that can come from some things. God says He will turn all things to good for those who love Him and are called to His purposes.

Man points to defeat. God is victory.

Believe and move forward. Drop the past at the empty tomb. Our Savior is not dead. Our Savior is alive, and His saving grace brings the dead back to life.

You are the one who can make the difference. Allow God full access into your life. Allow Him access to unhinder what has entangled you.

Are you carrying something from your past? The strong, loving, restoring hands of Jesus are waiting. Give Him your pain and allow Him to heal.

He Left Them for You

Tender with great care and love, He placed the rose petals along your walk, but you didn't notice or care.

He left them for you, the rose petal gifts, the beauty, the fragrance, the softness, He left them for you, but you didn't notice or care.

You hurried by His gifts, trampled, swept them away, even though they were left for you. The sunrise, the joy, the peace, the life He gave you, but you didn't notice or care. His heart broke as day after day He laid out His love, but you didn't notice or care.

He woke you in the night to talk, but you fumed, tossed and turned, then complained all day. His heart cried, but you never noticed or cared.

Every good and perfect gift comes from Him, and day after day He stretches out His hands, His eyes roaming the earth looking for hearts fully devoted to Him. His wisdom shouts in the streets. His unfailing love, a symphony tuned to the beat of your heart, calls and calls, but you don't notice or care.

God tenderly places the rose petal gifts for you. Oh, but will you notice, and care?

His heart cried and wondered when He returns will He find faith, and will anyone notice or care? Through crimson mercy from the Cross of grace, He offers to turn sins stains white as snow, because **He always notices and cares.**

Today, right now, will you take a moment to notice the things God has left for you?

James 1:17, Isaiah 65:2, 2 Chronicles 16:9, Proverbs 1:20, Psalm 33:18, Luke 18:8, John 3:16-17, Isaiah 1:18, Psalm 34:15

Unsheathing the Sword

During spiritual warfare I would pray in my mind about what was going on, asking for protection, guidance, and wisdom, but often I felt rather bloodied by the enemy.

One night I was under spiritual attack. I prayed for help, but then I felt within my spirit an urge to speak my prayer out loud. At first, I hesitated and wondered why that was necessary. Yet when the words were released into the air, the power came forth.

There is power in the words of God and power when we speak God's word.

I'm sure the enemy appreciated when I only prayed in my mind and kept quiet. I basically had kept my sword of the Spirit in the sheath.

The enemy can't read our mind. He listens intently to our words. The enemy bombards us with thoughts and constantly twists the truth.

Our words have power when we speak the words of God. Rebuking the enemy comes with spoken words.

Speak out loud God's word for His word is our protection and our sword. Once our sword is unsheathed God's power will flow forth.

Strength and power come from the word of the Lord -- use it for protection, use it for peace. The words of the Lord carry power, know them, love them and live them.

"Those who love Your law have great peace, and nothing causes them to stumble." ~ Psalm 119:165 (NASB)

In a World That Bleeds

In a world that bleeds, mourns, and dies, comes hope through the One who bled, mourned, and died. The love of Christ went to the cross to allow men to cross to God. In the darkness of a morning, in the throes of mourning, light shines in a tomb, and The Light walks free to free us into His light.

No matter how dark, how hopeless, and impossible it may seem, Christ brings light, eternal hope, and makes the impossible possible.

The wounds of Christ bring healing to the soul lost, the soul in pain and need. His nail-scarred hands are open to receive your scars. Jesus Christ, Immanuel, God with us.

In a world filled with evil, destruction, and wrongs, fall back, fall back to the arms of God. He conquers evil, that which is destroyed will be made new, and that which is wronged will be made right.

Sorrow taken to Christ blesses with the comfort of Christ. His love bled to cover you with His love.

In a world that bleeds will you accept the love that bled from the cross? Jesus offers mercy, soul-healing, and restoration. If you've accepted His grace and His love, please take His grace and love to a world that bleeds.

"For God so loved the world, that He gave His only begotten Son, that whoever believes in Him shall not perish, but have eternal life. These things I have spoken to you, so that in Me you may have peace.

"In the world you have tribulation but take courage; I have overcome the world. Come to Me, all who are weary and heavy-laden, and I will give you rest. Be strong and brave. Don't be afraid of them. Don't be terrified because of them.

"The Lord your God will go with you. He will never leave you. He'll never desert you. Casting all your anxiety on Him, because He cares for you.

"And He will wipe away every tear from their eyes; and there will no longer be any death; there will no longer be any mourning, or crying, or pain; the first things have passed away." ~ John 3:16 (NASB), John 16:33 (NASB), Matthew 11:28 (NASB), Deuteronomy 31:6 (NIRV), 1 Peter 5:7 (NASB), Revelation 21:4 (NASB)

Mind Spinning

Ever been trapped in a mind spin? The brain whirls and tries to process what happened or what might happen. Synapses fire like crazy trying to process what someone did, or said, or what we did or said. We wind up mind spinning on our problems, or someone else's problems, or the world's problems, until our minds are stuck in a downward spiral of futility.

Ack! Sigh...

Processing anything without God is pointless. Whereas, processing with God, points to God and His might and power.

In the Bible, David with great honesty would analyze his situations and circumstances. However, he always took whatever difficulties he faced back to God. Even when David didn't understand, he trusted God would do what was right.

When I sit and try to analyze something without my thoughts rooted in God, I'm just spinning brain cells. The Bible calls it leaning on our own understanding. "Trust in the Lord with all your heart and do not lean on your own understanding." ~ Proverbs 3:5 (NASB)

I know all too well leaning on my own understanding does not lead to pretty results.

When we moved to the Chicago area, we purchased a new home. Winter had not yet left, and our yard didn't have grass, trees, shrubs, or a patio, or anything other than a concrete step leading to cold mud.

Spring finally came and we were able to plant a few things, but we still only had those steps leading to the back yard. I could visualize a nice patio where we could enjoy sitting in the evening together as a family.

My sweet husband advised getting quotes from professionals. But my hubby traveled, and I was rather impatient. How hard could it be to build a patio? I bought a few books and half-studied the process. With the plan firmly partially half-set in my brain, I purchased the materials.

To prepare the ground, I decided a tiller would be needed. So, I rented an industrial-sized tiller. A BIG tiller. A **massive** tiller.

A male neighbor provided the muscle to wrestle the thing out of our minivan. I thanked him kindly and sent him on his way.

I love working on projects, and this one was no different. Okay, it was bigger than most of my projects. But how hard could it be?

I maneuvered the tiller into position and cranked up the engine. The mighty machine roared to life, and I released the handbrake. When that thing moved, it moved. I mean really moved. Blades spun at full-speed and the monster tiller clawed, tore, mutilated the ground and drug me like a ragdoll. Unable to stop, I rode that thing like a bucking bronco.

Finally, I was able to plant my feet. The behemoth ripped into the ground, sending seismic shocks waves through the neighborhood. I wrestled with that massive beast trying to stop it from digging to the earth's core.

A few miles from China, I finally succeeded in turning off the massive machine.

Collapsing on the ground, I surveyed the chunks, trenches, potholes, and canyons now mauling our yard.

Oh dear. My lack of understanding on how to work a tiller and how to build a patio were very obvious.

The only thing I successfully completed with that project was to entertain the neighbors. Years later they still chuckle about the tiller riding Buffaloe.

But I digress...

Anything we try to analyze without factoring the truth of God's sufficiency, might, power, love, and greatness, the less we will understand. Leaning on our own understanding is just mind spinning.

Whatever is troubling you, whatever you need to analyze, filter it through God's truth for the truth is found, answers are found, by searching in The truth with The One who is and has all the answers.

Turn off the mind-spinning and turn on the understanding with God's truth!

"If any of you lacks wisdom [to guide him through a decision or circumstance], he is to ask of [our benevolent] God, who gives to everyone generously and without rebuke or blame, and it will be given to him." ~ James 1:5 (AMP)

"Call to Me, and I will answer you, and show you great and mighty things, which you do not know." ~ Jeremiah 33:3 (NKJV)

Stop the shame and guilt

You know that thing you did? You know the thing that was done to you? You know the shame? The terrible feeling, the nightmares, the heaviness of guilt? Satan wants you to keep those negative feelings, carry those burdens, and wallow in the past all of your days.

I want you to know **the truth**. Jesus brings good news and is The Good News -- **you do not have to carry what God has freed you from**!

Jesus gives freedom from the past, freedom for today, and freedom for eternity. It is for freedom that **Christ set you free**. Whatever is taken to Christ is washed, restored, and renewed. Your sins have been forgiven and are as far as the east is from the west (Psalm 103:12), therefore there is no condemnation for those who are in Christ Jesus (Romans 8:1).

You don't have to carry guilt or shame.

I've had some rotten things done to me, and I've done some rotten things. Satan tries to hit me with a variety of past failures and difficulties. I have taken my sins to Jesus and repented and have been forgiven. The things others have done to me, I've carried to Jesus and He has healed my broken heart and bound my wounds. God has taken what the enemy meant for evil and used for good, and Jesus will do the same for you. Regardless of what you have done, or others have done to you, there is no sin too big for God to forgive. And there is no shame that too heavy for God to shoulder.

Jesus despised the shame of the cross yet took our sins and shame and nailed them there, and by His sacrifice we are washed clean. **Jesus conquered sin and death and rose again to give us new life free of guilt and shame.**

Don't listen to the enemy's lies that you need to keep living in failure, shame, and guilt. Run free in Christ!

"We are surrounded by a great cloud of people whose lives tell us what faith means. So, let us run the race that is before us and never give up. We should remove from our lives anything that would get in the way and the sin that so easily holds us back. Let us look only to Jesus, the One who began our faith and who makes it perfect. He suffered death on the cross. But he accepted the shame as if it were nothing because of the joy that God put before him. And now he is sitting at the right side of God's throne." ~ Hebrews 12:1-2 (NCV)

"I sought the Lord, and He answered me, and delivered me from all my fears. They looked to Him and were radiant, and their faces will never be ashamed." ~ Psalm 34:4-5 (NASB)

HELP!

Have you ever had a time where you really needed help from God but couldn't think of a prayer? Perhaps your situation or mood was so debilitating you couldn't even find words to pray?

Be encouraged, help is on the way. Pray, **H.E.L.P.**

Heavenly Father,

Everything is overwhelming me.

Let Your Holy Spirit please translate my needs.

Please.

Holy God,

Encourage me with Your love.

Lift me out of this pit.

Push away the sorrow with Your mighty hand.

Heavenly Father,

Examine my wounded heart.

Look on my soul with Your compassionate love.

Place me in the center of Your healing grace.

Hear me please, heavenly Father.

Examine my needs.

Lighten the darkness.

Put me in Your heavenly light where everything will become clear.

Remember when you need help, call out to God. Prayers don't have to be perfect or long. The Holy Spirit is there to help translate even our groans.

Do you need help? Call out to God, He's waiting.

"...the Spirit also helps our weakness; for we do not know how to pray as we should, but the Spirit Himself intercedes for us with groanings too deep for words." ~ Romans 8:26 (NASB)

"Our soul waits for the Lord; He is our help and our shield." ~ Psalm 33:20 (NKJV)

"My help comes from the Lord, Who made heaven and earth." ~ Psalm 121:2 (NKJV)

Fight Back

I've been in a battle; a long, hard, messy, frustrating, defeating, depressing, lonely, desert dry, hard, hard, hard battle with the enemy. Through prayer and God's word, I've made headway, felt the worst was over, then the enemy would hit again, and I'd flounder in misery and try to move forward, try to keep my eyes on God.

I sensed the Lord's Spirit telling me as a Christian I have the power of Christ. Not just a little power, we are talking THE POWER OF CHRIST.

As I pondered this truth, I realized God's power is always available to us as Christians because Christ lives within us. His power, His Word, His victory is available to combat against Satan.

When Jesus was confronted by Satan in the wilderness, Jesus quoted scripture (see Matthew 4). I can whimper and cry all day at the enemy, but when I quote scripture as Jesus did, that is when I find God's power. God's truth is our offensive weapon, our sword of the Spirit so that we can fight back against the enemy. (Ephesians 6:17). What is written is the truth and The truth sets us free.

I went to the Lord in prayer. Since God's truth is power, I took verses that applied to my situation. Throughout scripture there are verses that address our fears, concerns, and difficulties.

Nehemiah went to the Lord to ask for help, so I used part of his prayer to begin mine...*I beseech You, O Lord God of heaven, the great and awesome God, who preserves the covenant and lovingkindness for those who love Him and keep His commandments, let Your ear now be attentive and Your eyes open to hear the prayer of Your servant which I am praying before You now. O Lord, I beseech You, may Your ear be attentive to the prayer of Your servant who delights to revere Your name* (Nehemiah 1:5-6, 11).

I then used verses to apply to the address the areas where I was under attack. Whatever you are facing, wherever you feel the assault of the enemy go to God's Word and use your offensive weapons. As Jesus did with Satan, you too can respond with scripture to make the enemy flee.

Below are some examples where I took verses made them personal and responded to each issue. There are many other verses that will apply, this is only a small sampling. We are never left defenseless against the enemy.

If Satan is coming at you with feelings of loneliness – It is written... As the Father loves Jesus, so Jesus loves m (John 15:9). The Lord God goes with me. He will not fail me or forsake me. (Deuteronomy 31:6) Jesus calls me friend (John 15:15) God promises, "My presence shall go with you, and I will give you rest." (Exodus 33:14).

If Satan is coming at you with the feelings of being unsettled, not feeling at home – It is written... I have an eternal home with Jesus, He will be with me always, even to the end of the age (Matthew 28:20). Jesus gives me eternal life and I will never perish; and no one will snatch me out of His hand. God has given me to Him, and He is greater than all; and no one is able to snatch me out of the Father's hand (John 10:28-29).

If Satan is coming at you with feelings of Defeat – It is written... I can be strong and courageous; I will not be afraid for the Lord my God is the one who goes with me. He will not fail me or forsake me. (Deuteronomy 31:6) If God is for me, who is against me? He who did not spare His own Son, but delivered Him over for us all, how will He not also with Him freely give us all things? Who will bring a charge against God's elect? God is the one who justifies; who is the one who condemns? Christ Jesus is He who died, yes, rather who was raised, who is at the right hand of God, who also intercedes for us. Who will separate us from the love of Christ? Will tribulation, or distress, or persecution, or famine, or nakedness, or peril, or sword? But in all these things I overwhelmingly conquer through Him who loved me (Romans 8:31-37).

If Satan has people gossiping or backstabbing against you – It is written...No weapon formed against me will prosper; and every tongue that accuses me in judgment I will condemn. This is the heritage of the servants of the Lord, and my vindication is from God the Lord. In righteousness I will be established; I will be far from oppression, for I will not fear; and from terror, for it will not come near me. If anyone fiercely assails me it will not be from God. Whoever assails me will fall because of me. For God has not given me the spirit of fear (Isaiah 54:17, Isaiah 54:14-15, 2 Timothy 1:7).

If Satan is attacking your comfort and peace – It is written… Jesus gives me His peace. So, I will not let my heart be troubled, nor let it be fearful (John 14:27). Jesus has given me the comforter through His ever-present Holy Spirit (John 14:6). Just as a father has compassion on his children, so the Lord has compassion on those who fear Him (Psalm 103:13). The lovingkindness of the Lord is from everlasting to everlasting on those who fear Him, And His righteousness to children's children (Psalm 103:17).

If Satan is attacking your Joy – It is written … These things I have spoken to you so that My joy may be in you, and that your joy may be made full (John 15:11).

How is the enemy attacking you? Would you be willing to take time to find verses to address whatever you are facing? Speak God's Word, His Truth, tell the enemy what is written in God's word and the enemy will flee. For it is written… the word of God is living and active and sharper than any two-edged sword (Hebrews 4:12). And if you will continue in God's Word, then you are truly a disciple of Christ; and you will know the truth, and the truth will make you free (John 8:31-23).

Unified

Christianity doesn't mean conforming to fit in little boxes of a square labeled Christianity.

If puzzle pieces were only square, they might fit together and look alike, but there wouldn't be a linking point, nothing to hold them together. Shake 'em up and they are going to get all shook up.

With a link, a holding point, there is stability and unity. As Christians our link is Jesus. The beautiful diversity of the body of Christ is made up of every color, shape, size, style of haircut and dress you can imagine.

I'm so grateful my entrance into heaven isn't based on how well I can wear high heels or how fancy my dress. I need training wheels on high heels and only have only a few dresses in my closet. I'm most comfortable in jeans and tennis shoes. If only someone could come over and color-code my clothing for me, I'd be a much happier woman.

Thankfully God looks at our hearts, not our outward appearance. If we've asked Jesus into our hearts, we have the blessings of being united with Christ and with God. In that amazing grace-filled unity, we have the unity in the body of Christ. We are all unique people linked together through Christ.

Oh, what beauty when we embrace the diversity and uniqueness to look at the heart of a person instead of how they look or what they wear.

Let's link with Jesus to link with His love for nothing can separate us from the love of Christ!

"How good and pleasant it is when God's people live together in unity! Just as a body, though one, has many parts, but all its many parts form one body, so it is with Christ. There is neither Jew nor Gentile, neither slave nor free, nor is there male and female, for you are all one in Christ Jesus" ~ Psalm 133:1, 1 Corinthians 12:12, Galatians 3:28 (NIV)

I've seen some things!

When we moved from Idaho to Tennessee, we chose to ship our vehicles. The distance was over 1800 miles, meaning at least a twenty-seven-hour car drive, and trying to drive three cars separately sounded like a nightmare. I'm good for maybe an hour and then I get sleepy. Pulling over every hour to wake-up would have taken about a month to make the journey.

Sweet hubby flew in June to begin his new job. Our house sold in July and a flight was booked for me, our son, and the dog. Unfortunately, our dog was too big to join us in the cabin, and the airline wouldn't allow pets to fly if the temperature was over a certain temperature. So, we had to book our little dog on a separate flight.

Chipper had to be locked in an approved dog-shipping crate and taken to the air freight office in the morning on the day we were leaving Idaho. He could have food and water, but for his own safety he would not be let out until he arrived in Tennessee. We couldn't even give him a calming medication even though he would have two flights before he reached our new home. We prayed for him, and the man assured us he would be fine.

Unfortunately, Chipper's flight was delayed. When we were finally able to pick him up that night in Tennessee, we gently removed him from the crate and cuddled him, but he didn't even acknowledge our presence. He just stared with a thousand-yard stare.

Our son responded for the dog, "I've seen some things, man!"

I can't imagine what our little furry friend had encountered on his trip, but as soon as we took him outside, his tail went up and a bounce returned to his step. Whatever he went through, he knew he was safe with his family. He didn't seem to have any adverse repercussions from the flights, and now when we leave the house and return, we find him asleep in his crate.

What could have been a place with bad memories actually is his place of refuge.

We've all "seen some things." We all have something in our past we would rather forget, and wish didn't happen. We can't change the past, however with our Heavenly Father's help we can overcome our past. God takes the negatives and turns them into positives for nothing is impossible for God.

Whatever we've "seen" or endured, God is our refuge. With His grace, compassion, comfort, and love, we find healing, restoration, and renewal.

Please read the following verses and allow God's comfort for your hurting soul.

"He restores my soul; He leads me in the paths of righteousness for His name's sake." ~ Psalm 23:3 (NKJV)

"The Lord also will be a refuge for the oppressed, a refuge in times of trouble." ~ Psalm 9:9 (NKJV)

"Yea, though I walk through the valley of the shadow of death, I will fear no evil; for You are with me; Your rod and Your staff, they comfort me." ~ Psalm 23:4 (NKJV)

"In the multitude of my anxieties within me, Your comforts delight my soul." ~ Psalm 94:19 (NKJV)

"For the Lord God is a sun and shield; the Lord will give grace and glory; no good thing will He withhold from those who walk uprightly." ~ Psalm 84:11 (NKJV)

"He has made His wonderful works to be remembered; the Lord is gracious and full of compassion." ~ Psalm 111:4 (NKJV)

"Trust in Him at all times, you people; pour out your heart before Him; God is a refuge for us. Selah." ~ Psalm 62:8 (NKJV)

"I will say of the Lord, 'He is my refuge and my fortress; My God, in Him I will trust.'" ~ Psalm 91:2 (NKJV)

"Therefore, we do not lose heart. Even though our outward man is perishing, yet the inward man is being renewed day by day." ~ 2 Corinthians 4:16 (NKJV)

They Need to Know

Jesus told us to go and tell and make disciples. The world needs to know about Jesus. They need to know of The One who quiets the storms, who can do all things, who loves with an unfailing love, who promises to wipe away ever tear, who will never leave, who takes what the enemy meant for evil and will turn it into good. They need to know! Tell them. Tell them about Jesus.

Tell them what Jesus has done for you. They need to know someone who made it to the other side of grief, confusion, sadness, job loss, cancer, hardships, medical issues, family issues, issues with issues....

They need to know they can make it through. That's why I write. That's why I share some of the things I never wanted to share. I want people to know they too can make it through.

Everyone has a story; and they too have a Savior who loves them even with their mess and sin and deep needs. They need to know, and you can help. You can be there to point to the Savior.

I think sometimes when Christians are told to share the gospel of Jesus Christ, they worry that it's going to be a heavy burden.

The amazing, wonderful truth about sharing Christ is we are sharing a message lighter than air to a world unable to breathe.

Sharing Christ is shining the light in a dark world to bring the light of Christ.

Sharing Christ is showing The Way to heaven bringing life to those who so need true Life.

Sharing Christ is loving inviting others into God's love.

Sharing Christ helps them know God will be with them to help them through the tragic, through the boring, repetitive life, through the hard stuff, through it all. They need to know. You don't have to tell them only what you know, tell them Who you know.

Share Christ, He is Who you know. He will help you through and help others through. They need to know. Please tell them Who you know!

They need to know about Jesus. Who can you tell?

"...tell them what great things the Lord has done for you, and how He has had compassion on you." ~ Mark 5:19 (NKJV)

"Jesus came and told his disciples, 'I have been given all authority in heaven and on earth. Therefore, go and make disciples of all the nations, baptizing them in the name of the Father and the Son and the Holy Spirit. Teach these new disciples to obey all the commands I have given you. And be sure of this: I am with you always, even to the end of the age.'" ~ Matthew 28:18-20 (NLT)

Rescue

Our lives are flooded with information of the negatives in this world. We hear of wars, attacks, pain, and suffering. Rarely do we receive good news (especially on the news). But I want you to know that all over the world rescues are happening.

Rescues come through actions, words, and deeds. Rescues come in life and out of this life. Rescues are divine.

The slave is lead to safety.

The hungry are given food.

The refugee is given refuge.

The one struggling in pain is led gently home.

The reader discovers truth in the Bible giving eternal hope.

The soul lost and wandering finds The Savior's grace.

The prayer leads to breakthroughs, wisdom, hope, and healing.

Rescues are everywhere. I have to choose what I see and hear. I wouldn't be here if God didn't rescue. He rescued me through the hard times, and He rescued me from my sin.

Let's pray for eyes to see, ears to hear, and a memory to remember the rescues of our rescuing God!

How has God rescued you?

"He rescued me from my powerful enemy, from my foes, who were too strong for me." ~ Psalm 18:17 (NIV)

"The Lord will rescue his servants; no one who takes refuge in him will be condemned." ~ Psalm 34:22 (NIV)

"He rescues me unharmed from the battle waged against me, even though many oppose me." ~ Psalm 55:18 (NIV)

"Because he loves me," says the Lord, "I will rescue him; I will protect him, for he acknowledges my name." ~ Psalm 91:14 (NIV)

"For he has rescued us from the dominion of darkness and brought us into the kingdom of the Son he loves." ~ Colossians 1:13 (NIV)

Offended

We've heard of offensive wounds, but what about offended wounds? With the evil in the world, it's easy to get offended – offended at injustice, offended at pain we suffer or someone else suffers. It's easy to be offended at people for their actions and easy to be offended that God didn't stop the evil.

John the Baptist's entire ministry was dedicated to preaching and pointing to the Messiah. When he saw Jesus, John declared, "Behold, the Lamb of God who takes away the sin of the world!" ~ John 1:29 (NASB)

John baptized Jesus. John knew Jesus was the Messiah. However, John was thrown in prison, and he questioned, he wondered, and didn't understand. Through John's followers he sent word to Jesus asking, "Are You the Expected One, or shall we look for someone else?" (Matthew 11:3)

In the midst of heartache and tragedy, the human nature questions, wonders, and doesn't understand. How can these things happen? Were we incorrect in what we thought? God, are you still in control? In our pain the enemy taunts, "If God was good, He wouldn't allow *that* to happen."

Offenses and bitterness come easy in a world filled with evil. We can't fully understand, we don't see the big picture, the finished product, and the reason behind all that happens.

Jesus replied to John's questions, "Go and report to John what you hear and see: the blind receive sight and the lame walk, the lepers are cleansed and the deaf hear, the dead are raised up, and the poor have the gospel preached to them." ~ Matthew 11:4-5 (NASB)

Jesus didn't send a rebuke, instead he gave John a gentle reminder that He truly was the Messiah. And then Jesus said, "and blessed (happy, fortunate, and to be envied) is he who takes no offense at Me and finds no cause for stumbling in or through Me and is not hindered from seeing the Truth." ~ Matthew 11:6 (AMP)

The fact John was in prison was offensive. John's suffering and beheading was offensive. We can be offended at injustice, but we need to be careful not to be offended at God. Offenses are a stumbling block causing us to stumble in our faith and keeps us from seeing the truth.

Don't allow offended wounds to stay in your life. Offended wounds infect souls with the pus of bitterness, anger, and rage. They ooze with defensiveness, blocking the opportunities for healing. Offenses create gangrene soul scars that never allow the ointment of God's tender touch.

Hebrews 12:15 warns, "See to it that no one comes short of the grace of God; that no root of bitterness springing up causes trouble, and by it many be defiled."

The root of bitterness defiles one generation after another, spoiling with ill-will, destruction, and sorrow, destroying lives, families, cities, and communities. Don't allow a root of bitterness in your life or become bitter because of what happened to someone else (or is happening). Even when you don't understand, even when life doesn't make sense, trust God.

Drop your offenses and release your bitterness at the foot of the cross. Let Jesus have anything that has offended you and anything that causes you bitterness. Let Him carry the weight of the world's problems on His strong, healing shoulders. There is no pain, no heartache, and no difficulty too big for God. God will take everything the enemy meant for evil and turn it into good for those who love Him. God's justice will always be served, His love and healing are always available. Give Him your pain, your offenses, and your bitterness, and walk free in the light of God's grace, mercy, justice, and unfailing love.

Real Christians

The world needs to see real Christians, not just caricatures seen in the movies or on television. The world needs to see those who are truly living their faith in the truth and love of Christ.

I've had failures throughout my life; I've sinned and wandered away from God's protection, and yet God welcomed me back when I returned to His grace and mercy. I'm not perfect, but I serve a perfect Savior. Jesus loved me enough to pick me up from the slimy pit of my sin, wash me clean, and grant me a new life. He wants to do the same for you.

No matter who you are or what you've done, Jesus Christ offers forgiveness, grace, and mercy. Jesus is The Way to heaven for a new life and eternal life.

Christianity isn't just being a Christian on Church days. Christ followers truly live in the faith of Christ, loving Him and loving others, even on difficult and stressful days.

Christianity doesn't mean we're perfect, it means we have a perfect Savior who we love, and we want others to know our Savior.

Christianity isn't just saying words; it's about living life in Christ to show others the life found in Christ.

Christianity is loving Christ to show the world the love of Christ.

Share the real-life, real-life-messiness, of your life story before Christ and how He changed you from the inside out. Be real to a world that needs authentic and real Christians.

Tell them what great things the Lord has done for you (Mark 5:19).

Past, Present, Future

Once upon a time...

We've heard the fairy tales, the adventures, and the happy endings.

Can I tell you another story? The very best story?

In the beginning God created the heavens and the earth (Genesis 1:1). In the beginning was the Word, and the Word was with God, and the Word was God . . . and the Word became flesh and dwelt among us. (John 1:1, 14).

Now the story gets even more personal. Regardless of what you were told about your birth, in your beginning, you were wonderfully made, lovingly knitted together in your mother's womb by God Himself (Psalm 139:13-14).

Something else happened in the past. Jesus went to the cross and before He died, He said "it is finished" (John 19:30). He died, and three days later rose again. In the past, Jesus finished the work to set you free from your past, to set you free in the present, and keep you free in the future.

Jesus loved you from the beginning. He promises to be with you today and tomorrow. He knows the plans He has for you to give you a hope and a future (Jeremiah 29:11).

No matter what your past was like, your past had a beautiful beginning and has a beautiful ending in Christ. For God is preparing your eternal home where He will wipe away every tear from your eyes; and there will no longer be any death; there will no longer be any mourning, or crying, or pain (John 14:2-3, Revelation 21:4).

Rejoice friends, for in the past, present, and future, God is with you and will never leave or forsake you (Deuteronomy 31:6).

Good News, Please!

I enjoy social interactions and also time with friends, but often the sharing of bad news gets me down and makes me crazy. The world's a mess because Satan is very busy making a mess of this world. I don't need to read every article and every detail about some horrific crime.

Paul wrote, "Take no part in the worthless deeds of evil and darkness; instead, expose them. It is shameful even to talk about the things that ungodly people do in secret." Ephesians 5:11-12 (NLT)

As a Christian, my job is to share the good news of Christ; to share hope, encouragement, and light to a world living in darkness. I've lived through some terrible things, but God has restored and redeemed what the enemy meant for evil. Jesus Christ saved me! My God is bigger than anything or anyone! I have good news to tell! Will you join me? Please.

If we would share the good news can you imagine how encouraged we would all be? How excited we would be for the future because we would know our amazing God was doing amazing things. Oh my, if we would share how God is working in each of our lives, we would be having praise parties every moment of every day.

Please share good news. Share how God is working in your life. Share the hope of Christ. Share of God's mighty deeds. Share the praises. Share encouragement. Share good news. Please, please share The Good News!

"How beautiful on the mountains are the feet of the messenger who brings good news, the good news of peace and salvation, the news that the God of Israel reigns!" ~ Isaiah 52:7 (NLT)

"I have not kept the good news of your justice hidden in my heart; I have talked about your faithfulness and saving power. I have told everyone in the great assembly of your unfailing love and faithfulness." ~ Psalm 40:10 (NLT)

"Sing to the Lord; praise his name. Each day proclaim the good news that he saves." ~ Psalm 96:2 (NLT)

May I see your identification?

We all have an identity. Our passport or license contains basic information, but inside each of us we carry an identity, a label someone gave us, or we gave ourselves. I know many people who carry the wrong identification; they use their past failures, or the bad things that happened to them for their identity.

I have good news. You are not your failure, your sin(s), your loss, your divorce, your abortion, your victimhood, your illness, your family heritage, your job title, your difficulty, or struggle. What happens may hurt and wound, but don't allow anyone (including yourself) to define you by what happened. The only valid identification is who you are in Christ.

As a Christian, when God looks at you, He sees His beloved, sinless Son shining through your heart.

When we have given our lives to Christ, we are secure in Christ. Our identity is a child of the King of kings and Lord of lords. Even if a bad thing or failure happened after you were a Christian, your identity remains a beloved child of the Creator of the universe and Savior of the world.

In Christ, you are given the power daily to be forgiven, to heal, move forward, be restored, mended, remade, and recreated.

Moment by moment, God's compassion, lovingkindness, and mercies pour forth on His children.

Moment by moment God gives grace and equips you to walk through whatever you have walked through, and whatever you are walking through, and whatever will come next.

During my fight against Lyme Disease the doctors used PICC lines (a long, thin, hollow tube inserted above the bend of the elbow leading near the heart) to administer long-term 24/7 antibiotics. My body needed help to battle against the illness, and I was constantly and consistently plugged into my help.

When Christ is in our hearts, we are plugged into our ALL-powerful, ALL-mighty God. No matter what may come against us, God's unfailing love is already there to help us, fight for us, equip us, restore us, and give us every need for every need.

Now, when you think of your identification, always remember your true identity is in Jesus Christ -- eternally cherished and eternally loved!

The Next Chapter is Amazing!

When writing fiction, I tried to make sure each chapter ended with a hook, something to give the reader an intense desire to keep moving forward in the story.

However, sometimes we get stuck in our own stories. During difficult times, we think there isn't hope and there isn't a reason to keep moving forward. How often do we forget our stories aren't finished?

No matter where you may be, regardless of the stage you are in your life, your story is not over. Even when your time on this planet ends, your story is not over. There's always another chapter.

Paul wrote of running his race to win the prize and keeping his eyes focused on the goal. He reminded us there's more to come. For Christ's followers something wonderful is coming, and I can guarantee eternal life won't be boring.

Keep moving forward. Keep running the race even when you can't run. Keep your eyes focused on God and keep turning the page of your story, because the next chapter is amazing!

"Don't you realize that in a race everyone runs, but only one person gets the prize? So, run to win!" ~ 1 Corinthians 9:24 (NLT)

"So, we don't look at the troubles we can see now; rather, we fix our gaze on things that cannot be seen. For the things we see now will soon be gone, but the things we cannot see will last forever." ~ 2 Corinthians 4:18 (NLT)

"Then I saw a new heaven and a new earth; for the first heaven and the first earth passed away, and there is no longer any sea. And I saw the holy city, new Jerusalem, coming down out of heaven from God, made ready as a bride adorned for her husband. And I heard a loud voice from the throne, saying, 'Behold, the tabernacle of God is among men, and He will dwell among them, and they shall be His people, and God Himself will be among them and He will wipe away every tear from their eyes; and there will no longer be any death; there will no longer be any mourning, or crying, or pain; the first things have passed away.' And He who sits on the throne said, 'Behold, I am making all things new.' And He said, 'Write, for these words are faithful and true.'" ~ Revelation 21:1-5 (NASB)

What's Attached?

Have you ever noticed how heavy the air seems when someone is complaining, arguing, shouting, or saying curse words? What if negative words took the shape of clawed creatures that attached themselves to the person who voiced them? Yikes!

Be careful what you say to yourself and to others. Be careful what you mumble under your breath about your situation or another person. The Bible warns what we say has the power of life and death (Proverbs 18:21).

Words matter to us and to those who are listening. Remember Satan and his demons watch and listen. Don't put word ammunition in the hands of the enemy. Don't voice something you don't want crawling all over you.

Be careful with your words because every little word has consequences. Our words truly do carry life or death.

Now what if our positive words were fluffy white clouds that raised our heads and made our step lighter? Oh boy!

Speak scripture, sing praise songs, use your voice for good, and use your voice to speak life. Let's use our words to lift, encourage, and bring life to ourselves and others.

What words will you choose?

"Let the words of my mouth and the meditation of my heart be acceptable in Your sight, O Lord, my rock and my Redeemer." ~ Psalm 19:14 (NASB)

Discouragement Fever

I've noticed a very disturbing virus has attacked and left many feeling depressed and defeated. Discouragement Fever is spreading. I've had the fever, am trying to get over the fever, and have decided we must take action!

Since the first bite of forbidden fruit, this enemy virus has run rampant throughout humanity. However, there is one way to win this battle – inoculate with God's truth!

God's word contains the solution for every soul virus. Know God's truth and speak God's truth. We are in a battle. Battles are messy, but we know who wins the final war. If you are in Christ, you are on the winning team.

Regardless of how you feel, regardless of what soul-fever is attacking; remember God's might, power and strength are with you. You are never alone, never without hope, and always loved.

Do you have discouragement fever?

Tell defeat to beat feet and retreat. Banish discouragement with Godly encouragement. And remember the secession of depression comes with making God's word your possession.

"And you will know the truth, and the truth will make you free." ~ John 8:32 (NASB)

Bullied

The enemy is a bully and tormentor. You've probably seen him messing with you or with someone you love. You've felt the sting of words or the sting of blows. You've watched with your own eyes the evil in this world and sometimes it all seems too much. It's too hard to go on, and the enemy tells you to give up, that your life doesn't matter, and you should just walk away. Don't listen to Satan. Don't let him get away with what he is doing. Don't listen to his lies.

Your life matters. You aren't here by accident. God loves you and created you because He loves you. Regardless of what the enemy is doing, listen to the truth – God's truth. You are loved and wanted. You have a purpose. Every breath you take is for a reason. Don't walk away from God, run to Him because His love is waiting.

The Bible tells us to resist the devil and he will flee. That gives us the right to rise up and tell the devil "No!" and "In the might name of Jesus - Go away, devil!"

I was bullied in the past and the enemy tries to bully me with memories of the mess that he did to me in the past. I'm tired, mad, and I'm not going to take it anymore! I belong to The KING of kings, and I am a child of The KING. My Savior says I don't have to take what the devil dishes. So, I'm going to dish out The truth, stand firm on The Truth, and tell the enemy to go away!

Join me in stopping the bully with the truth of God's word!

"So submit to [the authority of] God. Resist the devil [stand firm against him] and he will flee from you." ~ James 4:7 (AMP)

If Satan is bullying you, stand on God's truth and speak the truth. Resist the enemy and he will flee.

Idolizing Grief

The other day something from my past came to mind, and I grieved. I grieved what was lost and what could never be regained. As I grieved, I almost felt guilty, so I asked the Lord if it was okay to be sad about that situation. I felt His gentle Spirit whisper in mine that it was okay to grieve, but don't make the grief an idol.

I've had some trouble in my life, however I haven't met a person who doesn't have sadness and grief in their past. Grief comes from the loss of a loved one, the loss of innocence, the death of a dream, or other heartaches and difficulties too numerous to count.

Yet through the comfort, grace, mercy, and love of our Savior we can find the healing for our soul wounds.

Yes, grieve the loss, but never make the loss the idol of your life.

The only One worth idolizing is God. He is the only one worthy of our worship. The enemy would love for us all to be stuck in the pain of the past, never moving forward, and never allowing God to heal.

God's comforting love is deep enough, rich enough and wide enough for any loss and any grief.

Would you take a moment to take your grief to God? Allow Him to comfort you as you grieve. Place your grief in His strong, loving arms, worship Him, and allow His comfort to wash over you.

Even in your tears worship God, for in the worship of God, our countenance is raised to look above the grief, above the attacks of the enemy, and into the comforting arms of our loving God.

"I love You, O Lord, my strength. The Lord is my rock and my fortress and my deliverer, My God, my rock, in whom I take refuge, my shield and the horn of my salvation, my stronghold. I call upon the Lord, who is worthy to be praised, and I am saved from my enemies." ~ Psalm 18:1-3 (NASB)

Worry Banishment

I found myself in the throes of worrying. As the worries grew, I decided perhaps I needed to take inventory.

Will my worrying actually help anything or anyone?

Does worrying about what someone else has done actually change what they've done?

Does worrying about what someone else thinks of me actually change how they think of me or how they think?

Does my worrying help my mind, body, heart, and soul?

Does my worrying show my faith in God?

Does my worrying help me remember that nothing is impossible for God?

Does my worrying show I love God with all my heart, mind, body, and soul?

Is worrying worth my time?

Is worrying worth my health?

Is the act of worrying positive in any way?

The answer to all the questions is **NO!**

How can I stop the worry process? I need to take my thoughts captive and replace the worries with God's truth and love.

So, I took and changed my questions into statements.

My faith in God's truth and love will actually help anything and/or anyone.

My faith in God's truth and love will help me focus beyond what someone else thinks of me and may actually change how they think of me and others.

My faith in God's truth and love will help me stop worrying about what someone else has done.

My faith in God's truth and love will show my faith in God.

My faith in God's truth and love will help me remember that nothing is impossible for God.

My faith in God's truth and love will help my mind, body, heart, and soul.

My faith in God's truth and love will show I love God with all my heart, mind, body, and soul.

My faith in God's truth and love is worth all my time.
My faith in God's truth and love is positive for my health.
My faith in God's truth and love is positive in every way!

Remember Worry is just a
Wicked
Onslaughting
Runaway
Rowdy
Yowl

Take your thoughts captive and banish those wicked, onslaughting, runaway, rowdy, yowling worries with God's truth and love!

"We use our powerful God-tools for smashing warped philosophies, tearing down barriers erected against the truth of God, fitting every loose thought and emotion and impulse into the structure of life shaped by Christ." ~ 2 Corinthians 10:5 (MSG)

Snatch Proof

Have you ever felt far from God? Far away and yet couldn't find the reasons for any distance?

I have.

I've repented of any and everything I could think of to repent, I've begged, pleaded, cried, whimpered, and whined, and still felt far from God.

Then I realized since I'm a Christian, Jesus lives in my heart, and if Jesus lives in my heart, He is always with me. And since I haven't done any self-heart-removal-surgery that means Jesus remains in my heart even when I can't feel Him in my heart.

Paul tells us, "And because we are his children, God has sent the Spirit of his Son into our hearts, prompting us to call out, 'Abba, Father.'" ~ Galatians 4:6 (NLT)

Jesus said we are snatch proof. "I give them eternal life, and they will never perish. No one can snatch them away from me, for my Father has given them to me, and he is more powerful than anyone else. No one can snatch them from the Father's hand." ~ John 10:28-29 (NLT)

No one (and that means even me) can snatch me out of God's strong hands.

If you are having those moments, days, weeks, months, when you feel far from God, remember the truth that Jesus lives in your heart, and you are snatch proof and safe forever in His heart!

Wounded But Healed

Friends, family, and acquaintances share their stories and prayer requests. The news reports illness, disasters, wars, and the cruelty of what man does to man. My heart aches for the pain others must endure. I don't have the answers, and in my humanity I can't fully understand.

However, I do know God cares and I know He has the answers and solutions. I know God hears our cries. I know justice will be served. I'm living proof of God's goodness—His sufficiency to endure, conquer, and live a full, joyous life through Him. I'm not alone. There are so many others who have been wounded terribly by life and now stand firm and safe in the love and protection of their Savior.

God takes the broken places and makes them whole. He heals, sustains, helps, and saves. His goodness, mercy, grace, justice, and tender love are waiting. No matter what you are going through, God is with you, will help you, and bring you safely home.

Would you be willing to take your wounded places to God for healing?

"My God is my rock, in whom I take refuge, my shield and the horn of my salvation. He is my stronghold, my refuge and my savior—from violent men you save me. Surely God is my help; the Lord is the one who sustains me. My flesh and my heart may fail, but God is the strength of my heart and my portion forever." ~ 2 Samuel 22:3, Psalm 54:4, Psalm 73:26

I Know What You Did

From a sound sleep, the thought came at 4:00 in the morning. "*I know what you did.*"

The memories of my past sins attacked and left me reeling. Embarrassment and sorrow grew until I remembered, **I know what Jesus did**! Jesus offered forgiveness, grace, mercy, and when I ran to Him with my sins, He cleansed me and washed me white as snow.

Then another memory came, and I remembered what they did – my innocence gone, and my heart and soul shredded. Yet I remember and know what Jesus did, He mended, restored, renewed, and recovered what the enemy had stolen.

Whatever has happened in your past, whatever you have done, whatever someone else has done to you, Jesus has done what needs to be done to give you a new hope and a new future.

When Satan taunts you with your past, remind him what Jesus has done!

"The Lord says, 'Come, let us talk about these things. Though your sins are like scarlet, they can be as white as snow. Though your sins are deep red, they can be white like wool.'" ~ Isaiah 1:18 (NCV)

"Who can accuse the people God has chosen? No one, because God is the One who makes them right. The Son paid for our sins, and in him we have forgiveness. Therefore, if anyone is in Christ, the new creation has come: The old has gone, the new is here!" ~ Romans 8:33 (NCV), Colossians 1:14 (NCV), 2 Corinthians 5:17 (NIV)

Scars Tell the Story

The other morning, I felt a tug on my soul as though God's unseen hand beckoned me to spend time with Him. I knelt in front of our fireplace with my Bible.

While I was praying, I sensed a need to polish our coffee table. I'm easily distracted, but this seemed different. The table looked fine, yet there was an almost playful thought that this urge was more than a cleaning project.

So, I started rubbing the wood with polish and a cloth. As I worked, truths became clear. The wood is beautiful, but the imperfections add character. The knots, rings, and scars formed by growth, environment, hardships, and trials bring beauty. The imperfections deepen and add a richness and glow.

Scars tell of the journey.

I have scars from my head to my toes, some scars have funny stories, some do not, and they all changed me.

Life leaves scars. Internal and external marks of what we've been through. Those scars are precious. They are proof of survival during the fires of life. They are rich, deep, and strengthening. They glow with the testimonies of God's faithfulness, because no matter how deep the scars, God's love runs deeper, and His love turns everything into beauty.

Scars tell the most precious story—the story of Jesus and His sacrifice for you. His scars prove His love for you. The scars of Jesus prove your life was worth the suffering to save your life.

Your scars tell a story. If you will allow God's healing, those scars become a testimony to yourself and others of the beauty of God's love. Your scars are beautiful when you allow Jesus into your scars.

Jesus "was pierced for our transgressions, he was crushed for our iniquities; the punishment that brought us peace was on him, and by his wounds we are healed." ~ Isaiah 53:5 (NIV)

Exposed

Have you ever had something nagging at your soul but couldn't quite see the problem?

I kept getting stuck in my writing and I asked the Lord to expose anything hindering my creativity. Then I remembered a comment from someone I had known. Stuck back in the recesses of my mind a statement a lady had made had wedged in my thoughts like a doubt roadblock. The lady had questioned how my daily writing for the Lord was even possible.

Ah, ha! The culprit was a doubt that had planted a doubt. In my own limited understanding, I was merely stumbling in the dark groping for a solution. Yet when I ran to God's light, His truth exposed the lie. God's truth exposed the lie reminding me that ALL things are possible for God. What is impossible for men is not impossible for God, because nothing is impossible for God.

Jesus is the light, the truth, and the Word which brings wisdom. When something is hindering you, bothering you, and you can't quite figure out the reason, turn to the light of Christ and ask for His wisdom to expose any hindrance in your life. As His truth becomes clear, God's truth will set you free!

Jesus said, "With men this is impossible, but with God all things are possible. I am the light of the world. He who follows Me shall not walk in darkness but have the light of life. And you shall know the truth, and the truth shall make you free." ~ Matthew 19:26, John 8:12, John 8:32 (NKJV)

Quiet Time

God wants to talk with you. It's amazing to think the God of the universe wants to spend time with us, but He does. You don't have to clean up your act before you come to Him. Jesus tells us to worship in spirit and truth, which means He wants to communicate in your spirit (your heart), and He wants you to be honest with Him, because in honesty, the lines of communication are open. God already knows our thoughts and yet He still loves us. God's love is truly amazing!

Don't be worried or intimidated by the terminology, "Quiet Time." A quiet time is not a time-out; it's a time-in with the One who loves you the most.

When we spend time with God, His word tells us, "You will make known to me the path of life; In Your presence is fullness of joy; In Your right hand there are pleasures forever." ~ Psalm 16:11 (NASB)

Through a soul-connection with God we find direction, joy, and eternal pleasures. Talking and listening to God is prayer, and prayer is connecting with the God of the universe, Holy, high and exalted, who desires a relationship with each of us (me and you). Wow!

For a quiet time, you can talk and listen to God, read the Bible, sing to Him, and basically hang out with the lover of your soul. Bible study and prayer aren't chores, they are delights because as we draw near to God, He draws near to us. When we read His word, His word feeds our souls. As we listen for God's voice, our ears are tuned to hear His voice.

The more time we spend with God, the more our thinking is transformed to think His thoughts. After spending months on a Bible study on the writings of Paul, I found my writing started to sound like Paul -- Grace and peace to you my friends!

Reading the Bible, spending time in prayer and praise, Bible study, helps us focus on God's amazing love, power, and grace, and keeps our souls tuned up and tuned in.

The Bible isn't a list of "do this" and "don't do that," the Bible is written to show us how God continues to love and invites us to a relationship with Him.

Are you up for a good spiritual workout? I love the Message version of 1 Timothy 4:8 "Exercise daily in God—no spiritual flabbiness, please! Workouts in the gymnasium are useful, but a disciplined life in God is far more so, making you fit both today and forever." What fun that a quiet time can actually get our souls in shape!

Will you take time to have a quiet time with God?

Cornered

What if someone was in the theater yelling negative comments during the show? "He'll never survive!" "She's a loser!" "No way this will end with anything good." That's what the enemy does with us. Satan is a tormentor and boy does he like to torment in the middle of the night when we can't do a thing about anything and are helpless, tired, and weak. The enemy doesn't fight fair and he's a bully. Grrrrr....

After a particularly heart-breaking time, I felt all alone, not sure who I could trust, as though I was a tiny girl standing in a corner with nose to the wall. I was battered, weepy, and tired.

Thank the Lord I then realized if I'm in a corner all I have to do is remember I stand on THE Cornerstone – Jesus Who is The Savior/Solid Rock/Redeemer/Mighty Warrior/Prince of Peace/Lord of Lords. I am never defenseless. And as a child of the King of kings, nobody puts His babies into a corner.

So, I turned around, put on my boxing gloves (sword of the Spirit style), and stepped out of my corner and back into the fight. This woman is a fighter who is on The Winning Team! And you are too!

God is strong and mighty in battle, the strength of our salvation, a stronghold for the oppressed, and a stronghold in the times of trouble. He covers our heads in the day of battle. So be strong and let your heart take courage, God gives strength to the weary. Trust the Lord, He is your strength and shield and will never leave you alone in any corner.

Feeling cornered? You are never cornered as a child of the King!

"Who is the King of glory? The Lord strong and mighty, The Lord mighty in battle." ~ Psalm 24:8 (NASB)

"The Lord also will be a stronghold for the oppressed, a stronghold in times of trouble." ~ Psalm 9:9 (NASB)

"O God the Lord, the strength of my salvation, You have covered my head in the day of battle." ~ Psalm 140:7 (NASB)

"Be strong and let your heart take courage, all you who hope in the Lord." ~ Psalm 31:24 (NASB)

"He gives strength to the weary, and to him who lacks might He increases power." ~ Isaiah 40:29 (NASB)

"The Lord is my strength and my shield; my heart trusts in Him, and I am helped; therefore, my heart exults, and with my song I shall thank Him." ~ Psalm 28:7 (NASB)

Beyond the Suffering

"Have you considered My servant Job, that there is none like him on the earth, a blameless and upright man, one who fears God and shuns evil?" ~ Job 1:8 (NKJV)

The most often quoted example of suffering is found in the book of Job. Job loved and followed God and had been blessed with a large family, wealth, and status. Yet with Satan's relentless attacks, Job lost everything – his children and all his possessions.

His reaction? Job fell to the ground in worship. Through all the hardships of Job, all his questions, wonderings, and pain, he cried for God to answer him and help him understand.

For thirty-seven chapters of the book of Job, God remained silent. When God finally answers, He never explains the reasons behind Job's sufferings.

Job's response? "I have heard of You by the hearing of the ear; but now my eye sees You." ~ Job 42:5 (NASB) He didn't get his answer to the questions of his suffering; he came to a greater knowledge of God. He saw more of God.

Trials and suffering strip away earthly thinking. If we will allow, if we will look to God, we will see more of God. The righteous suffer and yet will come through with the nourishment of a solid Gospel, the truth in God's presence, the strength of His arms, and the blessings that wait on the other side.

I don't know anyone who hasn't gone through suffering (or isn't currently in the midst of suffering). However please remember, in the suffering and beyond the suffering, the heart of God beats tender with healing, hope, and restoration.

Please remember God loves you. No enemy will have the last word or the last triumph. Even in death, we are victorious in Christ.

Please remember in the midst of suffering, God's tender heart is beating with His love for you.

The storms may rage, yet God will hold you close through the storm and joy will come. God will never leave you or forsake you.

In the suffering and beyond the suffering, joy will come. In Christ, joy will always come.

"Consider it all joy, my brethren, when you encounter various trials, knowing that the testing of your faith produces endurance. And let endurance have its perfect result, so that you may be perfect and complete, lacking in nothing." ~ James 1:2-4 (NASB)

"Not only so, but we also glory in our sufferings, because we know that suffering produces perseverance; perseverance, character; and character, hope." ~ Romans 5:3-4 (NIV)

"I consider that our present sufferings are not worth comparing with the glory that will be revealed in us." ~ Romans 8:18 (NIV)

"For just as we share abundantly in the sufferings of Christ, so also our comfort abounds through Christ." ~ 2 Corinthians 1:5 (NIV)

"But rejoice inasmuch as you participate in the sufferings of Christ, so that you may be overjoyed when his glory is revealed." ~ 1 Peter 4:13 (NIV)

Rocket Fuel

I've been under intense spiritual warfare, and at times the sensations and emotions seemed overwhelming and hopeless. One night I had a dream. I was in an oppressive darkness with the enemy closing in and surrounding me. With human vision, no escape was possible.

Yet when I spoke the words, "I trust God!" The rocky ground where I stood shot up from the earth far above my enemies.

Then I realized, trusting God is the propellant.

Trusting God is the key.

Trusting God is rocket fuel that propels us skyward above our enemies.

Trusting God releases the blessings of God.

Trusting God shoots us skyward to see more clearly our situation.

Trusting God releases the power of God!

Need rocket fuel to rise above your past, your present, or your future? Trust God!

"Blessed is the man who trusts in the Lord and whose trust is the Lord. ~ Jeremiah 17:7 (NASB)

"The Lord is my rock, my fortress, and my savior; my God is my rock, in whom I find protection. He is my shield, the power that saves me, and my place of safety." ~ Psalm 18:2 (NLT)

"For in the day of trouble He will keep me safe in His holy tent. In the secret place of His tent He will hide me. He will set me high upon a rock." ~ Psalm 27:5 (NLV)

"He brought me up out of the pit of destruction, out of the miry clay, and He set my feet upon a rock making my footsteps firm." ~ Psalm 40:2 (NASB)

"O God, listen to my cry! Hear my prayer! From the ends of the earth, I cry to you for help when my heart is overwhelmed.
Lead me to the towering rock of safety, for you are my safe refuge, a fortress where my enemies cannot reach me." ~ Psalm 61:1-3 (NLT)

Blessed by Blessing

The day after our furniture was delivered in our new home, our Internet service provider came to install the service. The young man, Alan, was beyond kind and helpful. He did an extraordinary job. He answered all our questions and went above and beyond a typical install by making us feel welcome to the area. He was awesome! Later my sweet hubby talked to the main office and shared what a great job Alan did for us.

A few days later Alan dropped by to check in and see how things were working. Then he told us how he had been personally thanked by upper management. They even played back my husband's phone call to share with him and the other workers. Not only did they thank Alan, he received a raise and promotion. Woo hoooooooo! I tell ya, that made our day! We are thrilled for him and still smiling.

God's word reminds us to be encouragers. "Let us think about each other and help each other to show love and do good deeds." ~ Hebrews 10:24 (NCV)

When we encourage others, we receive back encouragement. Alan was blessed and we were blessed to see him blessed.

We are blessed by blessings because blessings bounce back! Blessings are like flower seeds; they produce a beautiful harvest.

Bounce your blessings high, far, and wide, because every blessing God gives us that we share with others, bounces blessings right back on us!

Need a blessing? Look for who can you bless today.

"...always seek after that which is good for one another and for all people. Pursue the things which make for peace and the building up of one another." ~ 1 Thessalonians 5:15 (NASB), Romans 14:19 (NASB)

Surrendering

I've been pondering surrender and the death of self. Dying to self is a laying down of self to Christ, to be created new in Christ.

Surrender is a leaning into God, a relinquishing of the past, today, and the future. It is a prying off of fingers, letting go of self and surrendering self.

From death comes life. Surrender yields life. The seed that dies bears new life. The thorn bush bears roses. The desert yields a crop. Our healing leads to the healing of others.

Surrendering self allows a freefall knowing the fall will lead to death – the death of self which leads to new, eternal life in Christ. Death to self results in the death of fears of what was, what could be, and what may come, because self is now hidden in Christ. Surrender is freedom.

The Christian life is not about what you can get, but what you can give – your heart, your mind, and your soul to Christ. For in giving your all to Jesus, you receive His all – all to be who you were created to be, all to live life eternal, surrendering all to gain the abundant life in Christ.

Surrender of self = self-sacrifice yielding unfettered, undeterred, unhindered free-flowing movement of God's Spirit, power, and strength.

To be a Christ follower is a life that lays down self to exalt God. A surrendered life is surrendered to follow God. By surrendering our earthly weak power and strength we receive the Almighty power and strength of God!

Regardless of your circumstances, surrender to Christ and you find freedom. Will you surrender?

"Anyone who intends to come with me has to let me lead. ... Follow me and I'll show you how. Self-help is no help at all. Self-sacrifice is the way, my way, to finding yourself, your true self. What good would it do to get everything you want and lose you, the real you? It was for freedom that Christ set us free." ~ Luke 9:23-25 (MSG), Galatians 5:1 (NASB)

Feeling Woofy?

Tail down and whining, our little dog stood in the family room. He used to be a happy pup, back when my sweet husband and son would leave for work and school. I would go to my office for a quiet day of writing, and Chipper would sleep at my feet until the guys returned. He would greet them with wags and happy paws. But then things changed, and Chipper hates change.

Sweet hubby was laid off and our sweet son was home from college. The house was not as quiet. The routine became diverse, and Chipper couldn't figure out how to get us, and his routine, back to normal.

As I watched him muttering ... growling ... woofing under his breath I realized I had been just as woofy. I loved having the guys around, but I too missed the old routine. And I'll be honest; I wasn't good at waiting and often my prayers were more whining than praying.

I apologized to God. I want to live better by living in the moment regardless of the routine changes and any waiting involved. Because living in the moment, trusting the Lord, trusting that His timing is perfect, and His ways are the best, brings freedom, peace, and joy.

I want freedom, peace, and joy. So, I'm going to remember...

I don't have to worry about tomorrow because God is already in tomorrow.

I don't have to worry about change, because God is unchanging.

I don't have to worry about the waiting, because if I truly live in the moment I'm never waiting. Yay!

Feeling woofy? No need to worry, God's in control!

Pretend Christianity

The other day we watched a television show where a young man diligently worked for the main character. However, although this man worked hard, he wasn't really an employee, he wasn't even on the payroll. He only pretended to be an employee.

I wonder how many people are only pretending to be Christians? Perhaps they attend church, read the Bible, quote a verse here and there, say Christian phrases, maybe even wear the outward facade of Christianity.

They could even have good intentions, but yet don't want to live without "that" sin, "that" person and "that" relationship, "that" drug, or "that" vice? Are they only wanting to look good on the outside but living like (and for) the devil on the inside? They want all the feel-good kudos with Christianity, but really don't want to live a life of obedience to Jesus.

Jesus said, "If you love Me, keep My commandments." ~ John 14:15 (NKJV*)*

And, "Not everyone who says to Me, 'Lord, Lord,' shall enter the kingdom of heaven, but he who does the will of My Father in heaven. Many will say to Me in that day, 'Lord, Lord, have we not prophesied in Your name, cast out demons in Your name, and done many wonders in Your name?' And then I will declare to them, 'I never knew you; depart from Me, you who practice lawlessness!'" ~ Matthew 7:21-23 (NKJV)

Every time I read what Jesus says, it makes me tremble and makes me want to make sure that I know, follow, and obey my Savior. And I want to make sure all my friends, my family, and everyone else to know, follow, and obey Jesus Christ.

What price is high enough to lose a soul for eternity?

Do you want Jesus to pretend to save you or to save you?

A heart that loves Jesus wants to do the best for Jesus, because Jesus did the best for us.

Saying you know Jesus, maybe even saying you love Jesus isn't enough. Obedience is the sign of love. Jesus said, "If a person [really] loves Me, he will keep My word [obey My teaching]; and

My Father will love him, and We will come to him and make Our home (abode, special dwelling place) with him." ~ John 14:23 (AMP)

When we love Jesus, follow Him and obey Him, we receive not only His abiding presence, but the presence of Almighty God. And in the presence of God there is joy, peace, comfort, kindness, love, love, love and more love!

Pretend Christianity can't save. Be true to a Savior who truly loves you. I want to see you in heaven. I want you to experience, truly experience, the joy of true Christianity, true obedience, and true service to our Savior and Lord, Jesus Christ. I want you to hear, "Come, you blessed of My Father, inherit the kingdom prepared for you from the foundation of the world." ~ Matthew 25:34

There is no greater joy than living in the joy of Jesus, here and now, and for all eternity!

If you are unsure about your salvation, please make take time right now to admit to God your need for His forgiveness and mercy through His Son, Jesus Christ.

If you do know Jesus, follow Him, and obey Him, take time to thank Him for the beauty of His amazing gift of eternal life.

Lonely

Although I have a wonderful family and sweet friends, there are times I'm lonely. Not just a passing loneliness but a desperate, aching soul-cry loneliness.

I want to go home, really go home to my heavenly home. God is The One who knows me inside and out, who is never too tired or too busy to listen, who is never too preoccupied with life that He won't live life with me.

There are times I SO long for someone who will help me process through the process of living on this messed-up earth. I'm not alone in these feelings of loneliness. Even David cried out to God, "Turn to me and be gracious to me, for I am lonely and afflicted." ~ Psalm 25:16 (NASB)

Perhaps you too are struggling. The enemy wants you to believe you are all alone, that nobody understands, no one loves you, and nobody really wants to hear what's on your heart. But the truth is, God understands, God loves you, and He always wants to hear what's on your heart.

The loneliness that seeks to depress, press into God. In the loneliness seek Him, seek His face, seek His heart, and seek His word.

Lonely one, your heart is always at home in God's heart for "God makes a home for the lonely..." ~ Psalm 68:6 (NASB)

In your loneliness remember you are never alone. "I will be with you; I will not fail you or forsake you. Do not fear, for I am with you; do not anxiously look about you, for I am your God. I will strengthen you, surely I will help you, surely I will uphold you with My righteous right hand." ~ Joshua 1:5, Isaiah 41:10 (NASB)

The Art of Waiting

Waiting is not easy and is often messy and seemingly without rhyme or reason. However, I'm learning there is an art to waiting and waiting produces art. Sometimes the wait is a beautiful thing like a Rembrandt painting and other times may seem more like a Picasso.

The choice of the outcome depends on us.

By worrying, whining, and complaining about the wait, the waiting is difficult and messy.

In resting, trusting, and praising God during the wait, the waiting is nice and easy.

God's timing is perfect. "There is an appointed time for everything. And there is a time for every event under heaven." ~ Ecclesiastes 3:1 (NASB)

God knows the plan. "For I know the plans that I have for you,' declares the Lord, 'plans for welfare and not for calamity to give you a future and a hope." ~ Jeremiah 29:11 (NASB)

Resting, trusting, and praising God is an art mastered by remembering God's truth. Trusting God leads to the blessings of trust. "Blessed is the man who trusts in the Lord and whose trust is the Lord. For he will be like a tree planted by the water, that extends its roots by a stream and will not fear when the heat comes; but its leaves will be green, and it will not be anxious in a year of drought nor cease to yield fruit." ~ Jeremiah 17:7-8 (NASB)

Praising God brings us into the presence of God. "Enter into His gates with thanksgiving, and into His courts with praise. Be thankful to Him and bless His name." ~ Psalm 100:4 (NKJV)

Waiting on God gives us the power of God. "Those who wait for the Lord will gain new strength; they will mount up with wings like eagles, they will run and not get tired, they will walk and not become weary." ~ Isaiah 40:31 (NASB)

And the coolest thing God has shown me, is **if you live in the moment, you never have to wait.**

Listening

God is speaking, but will we listen?

God really does want to talk with us. Jesus said, "My sheep hear my voice and I know them, and they follow Me." ~ John 10:27 (NASB) If we are in Christ, we will hear His voice in our spirits.

God speaks to us through His word, through a preacher or Bible teacher, through moments of praise, through enjoying the beauty of His creation, through Godly insight from others, and through Bible studies that bring us closer to His presence.

When you read the Bible, ask God to reveal what you can learn. I love the Psalms, where I can find a fit for every emotion and difficulty. Psalm 119 is one of my favorites during times of hardship (just remember 911 backwards). The words are like a soothing salve.

Are you concerned and struggling with a situation? Write out your concerns and address each one individually with God. Talk to God. Listen for His response. Write down a verse (or the verses) that comes to mind or whatever you hear in your soul. What stands out? If you are unsure, ask God for clarification. Continue to ask the Lord if you have more concerns.

Cry out to God through the words in the Bible. Speak them to your soul and to your soul's Creator. Take the time to read the verses slowly, meditating on the truth you read. Make them personal and pray the passage back to God. Spend time with God, thank Him for the beauty you see, the blessings of the day, the blessings He gives with each breath you breathe.

As you are listening remember, *"God's voice brings peace. A sure sign that you have heard God's voice is that you are comforted and uplifted - encouraged to love Him, to trust Him and to follow Him."* ~ Peter Lord.

Remember God will never say anything that is against His character. "When the devil speaks, he makes us feel worthless and condemned. He nags and whines. He tells us we'll never change, that our repentance is not sincere. But the voice of God does not nag or whine or argue. It is calm, quiet, confident, and full of hope.

(Romans 15:4), love, (1 John 3:1), encouragement (Hebrews 6:17-18), and acceptance (Romans 15:7). He may convict, but He doesn't condemn. ('There is therefore no condemnation for those who are in Christ Jesus...' Romans 8:1)." ~ Teena Goble

God is calling to your heart; will you take the time to listen?

Come away to a desolate place and rest a while. Have your soul wait in silence. Jesus stands at the door and knocks. If anyone hears His voice and opens the door, He will come in (Mark 6:31, Psalm 62:1, Revelation 3:20).

Infinite Pleasure

The world says pleasure is found in possessions, people, titles, or fame. However, any pleasure found in the world is only temporary. God offers so much more.

Infinite pleasure is found in the infinite pleasure of The One who is infinite pleasure. "You will make known to me the path of life; in Your presence is fullness of joy; in Your right hand there are pleasures forever." ~ Psalm 16:11 (NASB)

Enoch walked with God and was taken straight to heaven because he pleased God (Genesis 5:24, Hebrews 11:5). Walking with God, spending time with Him is where we find joy and pleasure.

In God's presence our souls are plugged into the One who made our souls.

Our deepest longings are filled by the One who is infinitely deep.

Our desire for joy is joyfully given by the One who is joy.

Our need for love is completed by the One who is love.

Looking for pleasure? In the sweet spot of moving in tandem with our Creator, that is where we find **His** pleasure, and that is where our souls find infinite joy and pleasure.

Thank You Heavenly Father for Your unending joy and the pleasures forever found in Your presence!

I Do Declare

I absolutely love God's Word, it truly is alive, active, and always beckoning us to go deeper with our God. The other day I read a verse I've read many times, but this time something new jumped out. "But you are a chosen people, a royal priesthood, a holy nation, God's special possession, that you may declare the praises of him who called you out of darkness into his wonderful light." ~ 1 Peter 2:9 (NIV)

The Greek definition of "**declare**" (Strong's G1804) is to tell out or forth, to declare abroad, divulge, publish, to make known by praising or proclaiming, to celebrate.

How cool is that? We are to declare by praise, celebrating Christ and what He has done in our lives.

Jesus blesses us with His free, loving gift of forgiveness, grace, and mercy. In return we can pass on His gift by declaring to others what He has done.

So, I do declare to declare and publish the wonders of my amazing Savior!

Will you join me in declaring what Jesus has done in your life?

"My life is an example to many because you have been my strength and protection. That is why I can never stop praising you; I declare your glory all day long." ~ Psalm 71:7-8 (NLT)

"This I declare about the Lord: He alone is my refuge, my place of safety; he is my God, and I trust him." ~ Psalm 91:2 (NLT)

Rationalization Comparison

Be careful of the danger of comparing or rationalizing your sins by looking at the sins of others – the only measurement is by the sinless life of Jesus Christ. All (Every. Single. One. Of. Us.) have sinned and fallen short of the glory of God (Romans 3:23).

Don't allow sin to block your prayers or your life. Don't let sin block your walk with God. No sin is worth messing up your life here on earth. No sin is worth losing your eternal place in heaven.

Sin is toxic, grows, multiplies, and infects you and those around you. Don't allow, or coddle, or justify sin. Sin hinders. Sin confines. Sin limits. Sin takes away freedom. Sin is death.

Be repulsed by sin in your own life. No sin is well-behaved. ALL sin results in negative consequences. Sin is like acid, eating away at the soul.

Fortunately, God has the sin cleanser, the sin answer, in the mercy of Jesus Christ.

Want freedom and a clear conscience? If we confess our sins, God is faithful and just to forgive us and cleanse us from all wickedness. (1 John 1:9).

There is forgiveness of sins for all who repent. (Luke 24:47) Repentance is not just an acknowledgement of sin, but a turning away from sin.

With the power of Jesus Christ living in one's heart, no sin is too big or too hard for Him to expel it from our lives. So, fess up, turn away from sin, and face up to The One whose grace is greater than all sin – Jesus!

"If we confess our sins, He is faithful and righteous to forgive us our sins and to cleanse us from all unrighteousness." ~ 1 John 1:9 (NASB)

Restless

How can we find God's joyful pleasure in our restless world? When the soul cries out and thirsts and longs for a supernatural filling?

Even David cried out in desperation. "O God, You are my God; I shall seek You earnestly; my soul thirsts for You, my flesh yearns for You, in a dry and weary land where there is no water. As the deer pants for the water brooks, so my soul pants for You, O God." ~ Psalm 63:1, Psalm 42:1 (NASB)

In those desperate, restless moments cry out to God. St. Augustine wrote, "Our Heart is Restless until it rests in You."

As we seek God's presence, we can be assured He will draw near to us (see James 4:8). In faith, in trust, we can believe God's word, knowing that those who put their trust in God will not be forsaken. (Psalm 9:10)

In our need of God, we can come to Him requesting the desperate filling of our souls with His presence. Because in His presence, in the light of His love, everything else fades.

In God, we find all we need, all we want, and all we desire. Seek Him above all, love Him above all, and in all you will find rest in God's all-filling.

Pointing Fingers

I've noticed a rather disturbing trend on social media. Many (including Christians) are pointing fingers regarding the inadequacies and flaws of Christians and the church. Correction is important when wrongs are being committed, but where is the encouragement for those who love the Lord?

The world is discouraging, disparaging, and abusing the church and Christians, we don't need to give the enemy additional ammunition.

Jesus prayed for His people to be united in love. The Christian church is beautiful when we work in unity and encourage one another. Let's unite. Let's pray. Let's love one another. Let's throw off any hindrances that hinder us and the church.

Let's be encouragers. Encourage the people of Christ. We all need encouragement so that we may have courage. Every one of us have imperfections. Jesus Christ is the only sinless One.

Let's stop pointing fingers at other people's flaws, and point people to The Flawless One – Jesus Christ!

"A new commandment I give to you, that you love one another, even as I have loved you, that you also love one another. By this all men will know that you are My disciples, if you have love for one another." ~ John 13:34-35 (NASB)

"Therefore comfort each other and edify one another..." ~ 1 Thessalonians 5:11 (NKJV)

"I urge you to live a life worthy of the calling you have received. Be completely humble and gentle; be patient, bearing with one another in love. Make every effort to keep the unity of the Spirit through the bond of peace." ~ Ephesians 4:1-3 (NIV)

"Be kindly affectionate to one another with brotherly love, in honor giving preference to one another." ~ Romans 12:10 (NKJV)

"Therefore, let us pursue the things which make for peace and the things by which one may edify another." ~ Romans 14:19 (NKJV)

Fear vs. Freedom

Fear keeps us from freedom.

Fear comes by not trusting God will help in our life, the life of our family members, and those we love.

Fear comes by looking at the past without remembering God's mercy, forgiveness, and restoration.

Fear comes by looking at the now without remembering God is in the now.

Fear comes by looking at the future without remembering God is already in the future.

Fear comes by looking not far enough in the future, because in the end, the future for Christians is never-ending joy in heaven.

The Bible tells us perfect love casts out fear. When we live in the beautiful security of the love of God, we are able to live without fear.

Freedom comes when we remember God's perfect love.

Freedom comes by remembering God redeems the past, is in the present, and already in the future.

Freedom comes by remembering as Christians we have a joy set before us in the never-ending joy of Jesus!

Fear may come, but God is the God who was, and is, and is to come, therefore there is no fear when we remember the loving freedom in our Savior and Almighty God!

"The true children of God are those who let God's Spirit lead them. The Spirit we received does not make us slaves again to fear; it makes us children of God. With that Spirit we cry out, 'Father.' And the Spirit himself joins with our spirits to say we are God's children." ~ Romans 8:14-16 (NCV)

"Where God's love is, there is no fear, because God's perfect love drives out fear. It is punishment that makes a person fear, so love is not made perfect in the person who fears." ~ 1 John 4:18 (NCV)

Do not fear, for I am with you; do not anxiously look about you, for I am your God. I will strengthen you, surely I will help you, surely I will uphold you with My righteous right hand." ~ Isaiah 41:10 (NASB)

Fingers Crossed

Have you ever told someone something and they responded that they would keep their fingers crossed for you? Or perhaps even keep you in their thoughts?

I'm guilty, but then I wondered, what good is that? If someone has crossed fingers, they can't give me a hand. Thoughts are nice, but I'd rather be in their prayers.

Thoughts and crossed fingers don't have power, but prayer does.

Let's be careful how we respond.

Let's remember to bless others with prayer.

Let's keep our fingers ready to help and our thoughts filled with prayers!

"Devote yourselves to prayer, keeping alert in it with an attitude of thanksgiving." ~ Colossians 4:2 (NASB)

"Little children, let us not love with word or with tongue, but in deed and truth." ~ 1 John 3:18 (NASB)

"For the kingdom of God does not consist in words but in power." ~ 1 Corinthians 4:20 (NASB)

Pay the Premiums

If someone filled out forms promising to pay for insurance on their car or house, would that be enough?

If they told others they were buying insurance, would that be enough?

If they wrote about their insurance, would that be enough?

If they constantly visited the insurance office, would that be enough?

If they spoke at conferences, traveled the country, even recruited others to buy that insurance, would that be enough?

If they did all those things and more, would that be enough? Or would they have to pay the premiums?

Wouldn't one actually have to pay for insurance to have a valid insurance policy?

I wonder how many think they are going to heaven because they are "good" people, or grew up in a church-going family, or casually filled out a form, or even recited a prayer, perhaps even speak about Christ, but have never committed to obeying and following Christ?

Christianity is more than filling out a form, church-attendance, or being sprinkled at infancy. I shudder to think of those who will find themselves in this predicament.

Jesus said, "Not everyone who says to Me, 'Lord, Lord,' will enter the kingdom of heaven, but he who does the will of My Father who is in heaven will enter. Many will say to Me on that day, 'Lord, Lord, did we not prophesy in Your name, and in Your name cast out demons, and in Your name perform many miracles?' And then I will declare to them, 'I never knew you; depart from Me, you who practice lawlessness.'" ~ Matthew 7:21-23 (NASB)

Paul tells us to "work out your salvation with fear and trembling." (Philippians 2:12) Christianity isn't casual acquaintance, true Christianity is a life-long, moment-by-moment commitment to lay down your life to live for Christ.

Christianity is beyond action or head-knowledge, it is heart-deep, soul-deep commitment to follow Christ. In that beautiful commitment comes a relationship with The Prince of Peace, the fullness of joy, and eternal life.

When Jesus lives in your heart, your life is changed from the inside out through the touch of His love.

Jesus paid the premium sacrifice for our sins; all we must do is believe and follow.

Make sure you're committed, because being a Christian is one premium whose cost is worthy of everything!

Don't Miss God's "Every"

At times I've thought something was missing in my life, something I wanted or thought I needed. So, I'd stare and whine at the missing piece causing me to miss God's peace.

When the focus was only on what I thought was missing, I missed seeing God's abundant blessings. I had been so busy staring at one thing, I was missing ***everything*** else God was doing in my life.

How often are we so focused on what we think we need, while all the time, all around us, God is pouring out His blessings? How often do we miss ***every***thing that God is doing in all things?

Is there something in your life that has captured your attention? Ask God to show you how and where He is working.

God is always working in us and around us. His blessings endure forever, and His love never fails. Ask God to show you how to refocus your focus on His Kingdom perspective. Please don't miss God's "every" in all things.

"I will cry out to God Most High, to God who performs all things for me." ~ Psalm 57:2 (NKJV)

"Every good thing given, and every perfect gift is from above, coming down from the Father of lights, with whom there is no variation or shifting shadow." ~ James 1:17 (NASB)

Timeless Timetable

The "experts" on time-management block out time for every event, squeezing and managing every moment. What if we lived with the focus on eternity instead of the day-to-day, giving God our every moment?

The "experts" on child-raising, financial prosperity, and anything and everything, change by generations. What if we remembered God's ways are higher, better, and the right way for living throughout history?

The "experts" say we need a certain number of hours each night. What if we rested in the knowledge of the One who made us, the One who is timeless, knowing He will give us all we need?

The "experts" have books by the millions. What if we read, truly read, God's word to fill our souls with the living water and the bread of life?

What if we remembered God's word is eternal and relevant for every generation?

In the course of each day, we encounter times of good, bad, or ugly. What if we lived on God's timeless timetable? In every time, in every moment, God is in that time. There is no past, no present, and no future, where God is not already present. There is nothing in the times of your day that God is not in that time.

God is timeless. He is never caught off guard, or surprised, or unaware of what may happen. God is always capable and ready to equip you for whatever the times of your day may hold. God is there to help you through, and there to help you with every need for every need.

God's peace, comfort, mercy, and love are timeless to restore and redeem any time the enemy has messed with you.

God's word is timeless and eternal. There is no better expert, and no better way than God's way. His truth is always The Truth.

When we consider time in the light of eternity, time takes on a new dimension. Your life is eternal and timeless beyond earth's timetable.

Whatever difficulty you are going through, will not last forever. In Christ, our time is safe in His hands for all eternity. In the beauty of God's timelessness, He will wipe away every tear and make all things new.

Let's live, truly live, in each moment of His timeless timetable. For in all time, for all eternity, God's love never fails.

"There is an appointed time for everything. And there is a time for every event under heaven" ~ Ecclesiastes 3:1 (NASB) "Trust in Him at all times..." ~ Psalm 62:8 (NASB)

Who Are You?

Who are you? Not what you did in the past, not what someone else did to you in the past, the past is past, who are you today?

Who you are in Christ is a new creation, given new mercies every morning from a gracious God. Every day the old has gone and the new has come.

Forget the past by giving the past to The One who can heal any past. Run the race of today by fixing your eyes on Jesus.

You are a child of the King. Live today knowing who you are in Christ. Don't think that your sin is too bad or too big to be forgiven. God's loving mercies are new every morning and never ceasing. God is good to all, and His mercies are over all.

There are many who have suffered, many who have sinned, many who thought their past or their sins would keep them from living a full life. Yet the Bible and history, are full of examples of those who failed, of those who went through terrible difficulties, and who lived amazing productive Christian lives.

Don't sit on the sidelines or allow the enemy to sidetrack you. Run your race to win. Press on, press past the past, and reach forward to Jesus. Remember, if anyone is in Christ, he is a new creation. The old has passed away and the new has come.

Now, I'll ask again... who are you?

"Not that I have already obtained it or have already become perfect, but I press on so that I may lay hold of that for which also I was laid hold of by Christ Jesus. Brethren, I do not regard myself as having laid hold of it yet; but one thing I do: forgetting what lies behind and reaching forward to what lies ahead, I press on toward the goal for the prize of the upward call of God in Christ Jesus." ~ Philippians 3:12-14 (NASB)

Looking Through His Eyes

My friend has a tainted past. Jesus changed who she is now; her past has been washed clean and replaced with a new opportunity to begin a new life in Him. The past remains unchanged, but through Jesus, through His forgiveness and mercy, she is changed. Even when she told her husband and new friends about her past, they continued to love and accept her.

Unfortunately, ancient history, memories, and past perceptions cloud the vision of those who knew her before. Why do they refuse to see who she is now and who she strives to be through her Savior?

My friend is not the only one with this problem. How often do past failures cloud our vision? The past pollutes the present, which stagnates growth and change. We see what we choose to see in others. God sees the good in each of us, so much so, that Jesus died for us even while we were sinners.

We all require second chances. Michael Jordan was cut from his high school basketball team and yet he went on to make and break records throughout his career. What if he had not been given another chance?

Beethoven's teacher said he was hopeless as a composer. Albert Einstein did not talk until he was three, didn't write until he was seven, and was termed mentally slow and unsociable by his teacher.

Saul was a Christian hater and murderer. David was an adulterer and a murderer. Rahab was a prostitute.

What if they had not been given another chance?

God is the God of second chances and new mercies every morning. He asks that we love as He loves. "A new command I give you: Love one another. As I have loved you, so you must love one another." ~ John 13:34 (NIV)

God's love is for us all. Every. Single. One. Of. Us. That even means you. No matter what you've done in your past, if you turn to Christ, you are given a new opportunity for a new life.

The amazing cool thing about God's love is that His love is patient, kind, doesn't envy, doesn't boast, isn't proud. Isn't rude or self-seeking, isn't easily angered, <u>keeps no record of wrongs</u>. God's love doesn't delight in evil but rejoices with the truth. God's love always protects, always trusts, <u>always hopes,</u> and always perseveres" (1 Corinthians 13:4-7). (Underline mine)

We are called to love with God's love, and that doesn't just mean other people, that even means ourselves.

Look through God's eyes when you look at others and when you look in the mirror, and I promise you a new look at life.

"Accept one another, just as Christ also accepted us to the glory of God." ~ Romans 15:7 (NASB)

Proper Tuning

Just as a radio station comes in clearly when you tune to the proper channel, we have to train our ears to hear God's truth above the noise of the world.

Don't be like those who "grumbled in their tents; they did not listen to the voice of the Lord." ~ Psalm 106:25 (NASB)

Don't be like those who refuse to listen. "'And just as He called and they would not listen, so they called and I would not listen,' says the Lord of hosts." ~ Zechariah 7:13 (NASB)

Don't be stubborn and not pay attention. "But they did not listen or pay attention; instead, they followed the stubborn inclinations of their evil hearts. They went backward and not forward." ~ Jeremiah 7:24 (NIV)

Keep your ears open. "Listen, O my people, to my instruction; incline your ears to the words of my mouth." ~ Psalm 78:1 (NASB)

Remember God's plans are the best, so call on Him and seek Him with all your heart. "For I know the plans that I have for you,' declares the Lord, 'plans for welfare and not for calamity to give you a future and a hope. Then you will call upon Me and come and pray to Me, and I will listen to you. You will seek Me and find Me when you search for Me with all your heart." ~ Jeremiah 29:11-13 (NASB)

Keep your ears open and your feet ready to follow. "My sheep hear My voice, and I know them, and they follow Me." ~ John 10:27 (NASB)

Tune out the voices of the world. Tune into the voice of God.

Who Said?

Who said, you'll never be forgiven for "that" sin?
Who said, you've gone too far from God?
Who said, you'll never get over "that"?
Who said, you'll never amount to anything?
Who said, you'll never be able to accomplish your goals?
Who said, you're all alone?
Who said, you aren't loving?

Don't listen to those who don't speak God's truth.

God said...

I am forgiving, and I will wash you as white as snow.
Return to Me and I'll wipe away your transgressions.
My mercies are new every morning.
I heal the brokenhearted.
Nothing is impossible for Me.
I am faithful to complete what I started in you.
I will never leave you or forsake you.
I love you forever.

God's truth is The Truth.

Who will you listen to?

(Psalm 86:5, Isaiah 44:22, Isaiah 1:18, Lamentations 3:23, Ephesians 4:11-12, Psalm 147:3, Luke 1:37, Philippians 1:6, Matthew 28:20, Hebrews 13:5, Jeremiah 31:3)

Go Through!

How many times have you heard there are some things you will never get over? What's interesting about this statement is that whatever you are trying to get over, you've already gone through.

We don't have to get over any "thing", because no "thing" is impossible for God. That means every "thing" is possible for God to restore, redeem, heal, and renew.

We either believe God or we don't.

When Jesus offers forgiveness for those who believe in His name and truly repent of their sins, they are forgiven. When Jesus says He came to heal the brokenhearted and bind their wounds, He didn't just mean a partial healing.

I've been through some very nasty things, molestation by a baby-sitter, attacks, rape, being stalked, chronic illness, eight surgeries, and many other nasty things. The memories of those situations weren't erased, yet I know God has healed them (and is healing them). I know my Redeemer lives and I live in my Redeemer. I know everything I've been through He has equipped me to not only have gone through and survive, but to also live in a daily new life with Him.

God's mercies are new every morning. His mercies are there when a negative memory resurfaces. His mercies tenderly heal your internal and external wounds. His mercies turn around whatever the enemy meant for evil and turn it into good.

You are a survivor!

Whatever you've gone through, you survived. You are a gladiator who has been in the ring with the lions and tigers, and you survived.

There may be scars, there may be negative memories, there may be heartache and pain, but you survived. You are a warrior who survived the battle, and because you survived, you are here to point others to The One who helps us through every battle.

We don't have to just get over something, with God we go through!

"When you pass through the waters, I will be with you; and when you pass through the rivers, they will not sweep over you. When you walk through the fire, you will not be burned; the flames will not set you ablaze." ~ Isaiah 43:2 (NIV)

"Even though I walk through the darkest valley, I will fear no evil, for you are with me; your rod and your staff, they comfort me." ~ Psalm 23:4 (NIV)

Beyond the Box

I wonder how often I limited God based on what I could see with my own eyes or based on my own limited abilities?

How many times do I get comfortable (even in an uncomfortable situation) because the situation is familiar?

How many times do I squeeze into something determined to make it work under my own power?

How many times have I refused to step out of my own plans?

How many times do I not offer what I have, because I forget God has so much more in store?

God has no limits. His resources, power, strength, and might are inexhaustible. Our vision is too limited and too confined. If we only look at a situation based on our boxed-in ideas, we'll miss the vastness and grandeur of God and all **He** can accomplish.

It is in stepping outside of our comfort zones we see God work beyond our comfort zones.

It is in sharing with others we find the joy of sharing with others.

It is in venturing outside of our boxed ideas, thoughts, and reasoning, we can watch how God works out of the box of our ideas, thoughts, and reasoning.

It is in stepping outside the problems of today and remembering to be grateful and praise, that we find our souls uplifted.

It is in living in God's Spirit, we keep in step with His Spirit.

It is in keeping our feet on God's pathway that our steps are sure.

It is in stepping out of ourselves we step closer to His presence.

God often asks us to step out of our comfort zones and boxes to reveal new and exciting adventures. Do you feel that Holy Spirit nudge to stay in step with God? Step out with Him and watch what He will do!

Heavenly Father I'm stepping out of me to step closer to You! Please enlarge my vision and understanding of You so I may experience all You have to offer. Help me step out to experience exceedingly, abundantly more than I can ask or imagine. Help me to live beyond my own little box!

"...I pray that you, being rooted and established in love, may have power, together with all the saints, to grasp how wide and long and high and deep is the love of Christ, and to know this love that surpasses knowledge—that you may be filled to the measure of all the fullness of God. Now to Him who is able to do immeasurably more than all we ask or imagine, according to His power that is at work within us, to him be glory in the church and in Christ Jesus throughout all generations, forever and ever! Amen." ~ Ephesians 3:17-21 (NIV)

For further reading, see Galatians 5:25, Psalm 18:36, Psalm 37:23, Psalm 37:31, Psalm 107.

Break Through

In 1947, pilot Chuck Yeager broke the sound barrier. He reported the turbulence was terrible right before he broke through, but after, the air was as smooth as glass.

I wonder how often in the midst of major turmoil and difficulties if we aren't actually on the brink of a breakthrough. Satan wants to stop us. However, if we will keep moving forward with God's help, we can break through any barrier.

When times are tough, hold onto God, He will help you break through!

Though I walk in the midst of trouble, God will revive me; He will stretch forth His hand against the wrath of my enemies, and His right hand will save me. Thanks be to God, who gives us the victory through our Lord Jesus Christ. For nothing is impossible for God (Psalm 138:7, 1 Corinthians 15:57, Luke 1:37).

"If"

"**M**artha then said to Jesus, 'Lord, if You had been here, my brother would not have died.'" ~ John 11:21 (NASB)

How many times do we question God and wonder what would have happened **if** He had been there?

If that bad thing hadn't happened...
If my loved one hadn't died or left or cheated ...
If they hadn't done "that" ...
If I hadn't done "that" ...
If my job hadn't ended...
If I hadn't been raised in that way, by "that" person...
If God had (would have) ...
If God wouldn't have...

"If" lacks belief.
"If" blames instead of trusting.
"If" accuses instead of looking at what God does next.

If Jesus had gone to Bethany when He learned Lazarus was sick, he could have miraculously cured Lazarus. But because Jesus wasn't there, a greater miracle occurred.

Jesus said to Martha, "Did I not say to you that if you believe, you will see the glory of God?'" ~ John 11:40 (NASB) And then Jesus called Lazarus out from the grave. We're not talking just a little miracle; we are talking a HUGE miracle!

We can't see into the future. God knows what will happen next. God never wonders "if", He knows, and His perfect plans will come to pass for our good and His glory.

Think of the people throughout history who became heroes, whose stories we tell, whose walk we admire, who have gone through terrible trials and suffering. If they had been kept from those difficulties, we (and they) would never have experienced God's glory.

All those times I wondered about the "what if's" in my own life and wondered what would be different, now I can look back and see all the ways God has restored, redeemed, and used it all for good and His glory.

So, the next time you're wondering about the "if" in your life, remember to believe, and you too will see the glory of God.

Inversion

During the winter months, when we lived in Boise, Idaho, the colder air would at times be trapped in an inversion. Warm air would rise, and the cold air descended into the valley. The clouds would settle in a foggy soup, vision was clouded, it was cold, and the more the pollution built, the heavier and more toxic the air. Yet if you drove up the mountains, the air would be clear, warmer, and the sun would be shining.

In this world, it's easy for our minds to be fogged by the toxicity of life's difficulties. Yet if we will rise up and focus on The Son, He is always shining to burn away the fog of discouragement, disillusionment, and despair.

If your life seems dreary and foggy, look to Jesus – the everlasting, ever-shining Son!

"Arise, shine; for your light has come, and the glory of the Lord has risen upon you." ~ Isaiah 60:1 (NASB)

Safety

The last year I've had repeated dreams about different people trying unsuccessfully to kill me. My website was under attack from hackers, and I also received a threatening message. I haven't been fearful about these dreams and issues; I'm just not sure if these are warnings of things to come or warnings to be cautious.

We moved from an area with a very low crime rate to an area with a very high crime rate. For months the Lord had stirred in my spirit He was moving us. When the door opened, we knew this was His move. However, it was up to us to follow.

Human logic says follow the safest path. But the Bible warns in Proverbs 14:12 and Proverbs 16:25 -- "There is a way which seems right to a man, but its end is the way of death." ~ Proverbs 14:12 (NASB), Proverbs 16:25 (NASB) The only right way is to follow God.

Following God's lead is what we chose, because the only safety, the very safest place, is to follow God. Does that mean we are guaranteed personal or property safety? Maybe, maybe not. However, I do know obedience leads to blessings and by obeying God's leading I know we always have soul safety. As for me and my house, we will follow and serve the Lord.

I love God. I want to follow Him wherever He leads, because in the fiery furnace is where God shines. In the darkest nights God's light is even more visible. Even as storms rage, we can curl up and rest with Jesus.

Once we settled in our new state, we found amazing, wonderful, Godly people. We found a church home, and we are experiencing wonderful ways the Lord works, because our Lord is always working.

Remember, Christian's aren't only soul-safe, we are invincible. We can live fearless in Christ, because our eternal safe place is in God who is our eternal safety.

"The name of the Lord is a strong tower; the righteous runs into it and is safe." ~ Proverbs 18:10 (NASB)

"In peace I will both lie down and sleep, for You alone, O Lord, make me to dwell in safety." ~ Psalm 4:8 (NASB)

"So be strong and courageous! Do not be afraid and do not panic before them. For the Lord your God will personally go ahead of you. He will neither fail you nor abandon you." ~ Deuteronomy 31:6 (NLT)

Through the Haze

Have you ever been with someone, and you could tell something wasn't quite right? No matter how you tried to find a reason, you just couldn't find out what was causing an uncomfortable feeling.

My analysis of trying to understand without any divine understanding is just a waste of time. It's like a dog chasing his tail, even if he catches it, he isn't going anywhere.

I'm tired of some "thing" blocking my path, messing with my brain, and causing me to wonder what I could do differently, what I had done, what my friend had done, and what had happened. Sometimes the enemy is trying to block us, cause us to stumble, mess with us, or create problems in the body of Christ.

Regardless of the smoky haze of disharmony the enemy is trying to stir up, God's truth is clear as the light of a billion suns. I'm going to move forward with God's truthful love. God tells us to love with His love, not love when we have everything figured out about ourselves and others. His love flows freely 24/7 from His throne to give us His love to share His love. It's not a love we have to manufacture. God's love is an inexhaustible supply.

God's supply of love is patient, kind, not jealous, doesn't brag, isn't arrogant, doesn't act unbecomingly, doesn't seek its own, isn't provoked, and doesn't take into account a wrong suffered, doesn't rejoice in unrighteousness, rejoices with the truth, bears all things, believes all things, hopes all things, and never fails.

Through the journey of life, I don't want to miss a moment. I don't want to miss God's best. I don't want anything to hold me back (especially me) when it comes to following God.

I'm going to step over, step aside, step around, and step through whatever is hindering. I can love with God's love. I can stop trying to analyze, and wonder, and worry, I can lay the haze in God's strong, trustworthy, loving hands and ask Him to love through me.

If we don't step out of our comfort zone, over our problems, in line with God, through (or around) whatever fear/good thing/bad thing holds us back. And follow God's ways. What will we miss?

Heavenly Father, help me to take whatever is happening to You. Help me to love with Your love and step over, aside, around, and through whatever smoke screen the enemy has tried to blow in my face. I don't want to miss anything You have for me. Help me to always follow You. Help me to ignore the haze and walk in the clarity of Your loving light to love fully with Your love.

Heavenly Father, teach me Your laws, and I will always follow them (Psalm 119:33).

Let's

Let's forgive in the same way Jesus offers forgiveness.

Let's stop whining about our wounds and instead praise our Savior who heals all wounds.

Let's stop focusing on the past and instead look to the eternal future.

Let's stop looking at the darkness and instead shine the light on the One who is light.

Let's offer grace like Jesus offers grace.

Let's love in the same way we are loved by Jesus.

Let's live, truly live as Christians.

Let's love one another, for love is from God (1 John 4:7).

If we live by the Spirit, let's also walk by the Spirit (Galatians 5:25).

While we have opportunity, let's do good to all people, and especially to those who are of the household of the faith (Galatians 6:10).

Let's love like Jesus!

Burning the Hindrances

I've been feeling SO hindered. Miserably hindered. Whiny, needy, MISERABLY hindered. I couldn't figure out some of the things hindering and burdening my soul.

I wrote down the things that were concerning me. Then I prayed over them, gave them to the Lord, ripped them up, and placed them in a candle flame. I watched the paper burn, and I prayed and released them to God. And I felt relieved. Free. Lighter. Cleaner.

Is something burdening or hindering you? May I humbly suggest talking with God and then giving Him those burdens? God wants you to be unhindered. He's waiting and ready to shoulder every concern and rid every hindrance. Burn the hindrances in the flame of God's love.

"Cast your burden upon the Lord and He will sustain you; He will never allow the righteous to be shaken. For My yoke is easy and My burden is light. Therefore, also now, says the Lord, turn and keep on coming to Me with all your heart, with fasting, with weeping, and with mourning [until every hindrance is removed, and the broken fellowship is restored]." ~ Psalm 55:22 (NASB), Matthew 11:30 (NASB), Joel 2:12 (AMP)

1000 Springs

Idaho may be known for potatoes; however, the diversity of the landscape is amazing. The state contains scenery resembling the moon, towering mountains, rivers, canyons, waterfalls, hot springs, miles of sagebrush wilderness, ski resorts, sand dunes, deserted gold-rush towns, and ruts marking the trail of wagons from the 1800's crossing to travel west.

Underneath the eastern Snake River plain is an aquifer covering an area as large as Lake Erie. The water runs silent and undisturbed until it pours out in canyons, waterfalls, and rivers.

Near the town of Hagerman, out of seemingly solid rock, water gushes out in 1000 springs. What couldn't be seen becomes seen.

There are times God remains silent as we wait for His guidance and His perfect timing on the next steps. Yet underneath, in places unseen, God works.

If you are in a season of silence, hold fast to God's truth. His living water trickles, flows, squirts, and gushes, remaining constant in the unfailing love of God. In the silence of the world's troubles, remember God will punish those who do evil. Even in the silence, hold fast to the reality God remains in control, God continues to move, and God will guide and lead through the desert times.

"And the Lord will continually guide you, and satisfy your desire in scorched places, and give strength to your bones; and you will be like a watered garden, and like a spring of water whose waters do not fail." Jesus said, "He who believes in Me, as the Scripture said, 'From his innermost being will flow rivers of living water.'" ~ Isaiah 58:11 (NASB), John 7:38 (NASB)

Storms

Severance dwindled, insurance ended soon, and we were 168 days into my sweet husband's job outsourcing, and still the wait continued. The waves of questions pummeled as we prayed, searched for work, and waited for God to calm the storm.

The disciples understood this concept. Jesus sent them ahead early in the evening to cross the lake. Then the storm hit. Scholars estimate the disciples struggled against a raging tempest for close to nine hours. Their boat mercilessly pounded by wind and rain and battered by waves. Every muscle on their bodies taxed to the limit as they struggled, rowed, and prayed for help.

Then finally in the fourth watch of the night, Jesus went to them, walking on the sea, telling them not to be afraid, take courage, "I am here!" (Matthew 14:25 - 27).

Are you in a storm? No matter how high the waves, or how strong the winds, don't be afraid, take courage, Jesus is with you to rescue and save. No storm is too big; no waves are too wild, no night too dark for your Savior to save.

"Do not be afraid or discouraged, for the Lord will personally go ahead of you. He will be with you; he will neither fail you nor abandon you." ~ Deuteronomy 31:8 (NLT)

Proper Vision

My eyesight changed again, and my poor eyes were struggling. Without corrective lenses, my vision is terribly flawed. Fortunately, the doctor helped me receive the proper prescription.

I can't just buy a pair of glasses off the rack, can't borrow a friend's reading glasses, or even use ones I've had in the past. My eyes need to be given the correct lenses for the proper vision.

In the same way, we have to make sure we see through God's truth.

There are those who say, "This is how I see, so you also should see my way." Even the media has power for good or evil based on how they report. The angle of the camera can be used to sway public opinion.

Editors can edit video and audio to present what they want you to see and hear. People can do the same by only giving information to help their cause or further their agenda.

Churches, friendships, families, and countries have split from inaccurate vision.

Are you basing how you react and act, or what you think about a situation or person, on how someone else told you to see?

Be careful. Be wise. Be committed to God and His truth, because His truth sets you free. His truth gives clarity. His truth keeps us unified in His love.

Please remember the only way to truly see seeing through God's truth.

Heavenly Father, open our eyes to see clearly and live by Your truth. Help us to see things Your way above all other ways. Please correct our vision to Your proper vision.

"Jesus used a picture-story as He spoke to them. He said, 'Can one blind man lead another blind man? Will they not fall into the ditch together?'" ~ Luke 6:39 (NLV)

"Where there is no vision, the people are unrestrained, but happy is he who keeps the law." ~ Proverbs 29:18 (NASB)

"How blessed is the man who does not walk in the counsel of the wicked, nor stand in the path of sinners, nor sit in the seat of scoffers! But his delight is in the law of the Lord, and in His law he meditates day and night." ~ Psalm 1:1-2 (NASB)

Seeing Beyond Ordinary

I don't want to miss how God is working. I don't want to be limited by earthly vision. Every moment of every day God is working in extraordinary ways to reveal His glory, but only a few are watching.

Two thousand years ago the heavens had been silent for so very long and then an ordinary young virgin and an ordinary carpenter were chosen to be part of a very extraordinary event.

The extraordinary became ordinary, and a tiny baby squirmed and cried in the midst of a dirty stable. Jesus Christ, born in Bethlehem. No fanfare, no paparazzi, no entourage, no castle for a King, just a seemingly ordinary baby. Angels and all creation watched in awe, yet so few people noticed anything so very ordinary.

But there were those who sought God, watched, read His word, and listened.

The shepherds watching their sheep, heard the message of an extraordinary event, and they ran to worship.

Eight days after his birth, Jesus was taken to the temple by Joseph and Mary to present an offering. They only had a very poor offering for they were very poor, just an ordinary couple. Yet an elderly man, Simeon, saw them, he saw the baby and Simeon worshiped Jesus. Simeon saw beyond the ordinary because he had been looking, watching, and waiting for the Messiah, for the consolation of Israel, the comfort of Israel, the fulfillment of extraordinary love.

An eighty-four-year-old widow, Anna, also saw, rejoiced, and worshiped.

The Magi from the east watched and followed an extraordinary star, traveling far to find a king in ordinary flesh, and they worshiped.

Simeon and Anna, the Magi, the shepherds, saw Jesus, they saw through the ordinary. They were the ones who noticed and experienced the joy and fellowship with their Savior.

Truth is revealed to those who watch and seek. Truth comes through the Holy Spirit who testifies and reveals beyond what mortal eyes can see.

Jesus is the truth, the life, the light. His grace gifts us to live far from ordinary lives because our hearts carry an extraordinary Savior.

Believe and be one who watches, seeks, and sees beyond the ordinary to notice the glory of an extraordinary God.

"Jesus said to her, 'Did I not say to you that if you believe, you will see the glory of God?'" ~ John 11:40 (NASB)

Reasons to Smile

Smiling today as I think of these facts...

God is full of Grace. His grace can wash any sin and every sinner clean.

God is a merciful God. He meets the sinner where they are and offers mercy.

God is a loving God. His love knows no bounds and is unfailing.

God comforts. His comfort meets in the depth of the deepest grief.

God meets needs. Whatever needs you are needing; God is able to meet that need.

God listens. He hears when you call.

God is able. Nothing is impossible for God.

God strengthens. No matter how weak you may be, God's strength never fails.

God won't leave you. He is timeless and is in whatever time and whatever place you are.

God restores and redeems. Whatever you have lost, God restores and redeems.

God wins. There is nothing you have been through (or will go through) that God will not help you through. The battles will come but the final war is won, and at the end for those who are in Christ Jesus, they will receive a happy, forever ending.

And that small list is only a drop in the bucket.

Need a reason to smile? Remember, God loves you!

What can you add to the list?

Bold Future

It's so easy to look at the past, or today's problems, or the worries about the future. However, anytime I focus on something other than our Savior, I've focused on something (or someone) that can't save. When I spend my time trying to analyze or fix a situation (or person), I've wasted my time. I must keep my eyes fixed on Jesus.

Concerns and worries are deflating, but a life focused on Jesus is inflated with His power, truth, life, and His love.

Life is full of obstacles and hindrances. There's gonna be trouble in the world, but we have a Savior who has overcome the world!

Strength and power for the past, present, and future, is found in The One who is strength and power.

Future hope is found in The One who is our future and our hope.

God knows the plans for our life, plans for welfare and not calamity to give us a future and a hope. So, let's lay aside every hindrance and any sin that entangles us. And let's run our race with endurance, fixing our eyes on Jesus who is sitting at the right hand of God.

I'm fixing my eyes on Jesus, throwing off the hindrances, and boldly running the race into my future with The One who holds my future!

Join me? Let's step (or run) into our bold future!

See John 16:33, Jeremiah 29:11, Hebrews 12:1-2

The Ending

Jesus received word Lazarus was sick, "But when Jesus heard this, He said, 'This sickness is not to end in death, but for the glory of God, so that the Son of God may be glorified by it." ~ John 11:4 (NASB)

Lazarus did die, but his death wasn't the end. Jesus raised Lazarus from the dead and that is the promise for all of us who believe and put their trust in Jesus Christ -- death will never be the ending. Jesus is the resurrection to new life. **For Christians death is not and end** but a new beginning.

Death is a step into paradise for those who love the Lord. Death is a step into glory!

Christians don't have to fear the ending because the only thing that ends is our mortal bodies. Once we slough off the flesh suit, we live forever in a new body that never decays, where pain doesn't exist, and tears are only shed in pure delight.

For Christ's follower's death is an ending to the heartaches of this world to step into the unending joys of eternity!

If you love Jesus, you never have to fear the ending.

Run to Win

Hebrews 12:1-2 and 1 Corinthians 9:24, tells us to run the race to win the prize by laying aside anything that hinders so we can run with endurance the race set before us, fixing our eyes on Jesus.

I'm a visual learner so I envision a huge athletic track. On it are several large groups of runners clumped together, lots of smaller groups travel together, but most runners are quietly running alone. There are even a few who sit in the track and trip up other runners. Others sit faced forward and some sit faced backwards, blocking and hindering other runners. Occasionally someone will stop and lift up the squatters, gently prodding and encouraging them forward.

I think I've been in all those categories. At times I've sat starting backward at my past, unable to move forward, even perhaps hindering others as I bemoaned all the bad things that happened. Then even when I stood on my feet, I still didn't quite make it into the race. At times I've tried to connect with a large group, looking at them instead of Jesus.

Yet when I fixed my eyes on Jesus, when I focused squarely on Him, then I could run with abandon, leave the past behind, run in my own lane, free and unhindered!

So, my questions for all of us...

Are we so preoccupied with the past that we are sitting and squatting instead of facing forward and running?

Do we hinder or encourage other runners?

Are we stumbling over the past instead of running free?

Do we look at the other runners, the other groups, instead of looking to Jesus?

Are we running our individual race, the race God has for us?

Will we fix our eyes squarely on Jesus and run with abandon?

Let's run free, friends! Let's run to win!

"Do you not know that those who run in a race all run, but only one receives the prize? Run in such a way that you may win."
~ 1 Corinthians 9:24 (NASB)

"Therefore, since we have so great a cloud of witnesses surrounding us, let us also lay aside every encumbrance and the sin which so easily entangles us, and let us run with endurance the race that is set before us, fixing our eyes on Jesus, the author and perfecter of faith, who for the joy set before Him endured the cross, despising the shame, and has sat down at the right hand of the throne of God." ~ Hebrews 12:1-2 (NASB)

Run Back!

Jesus offers forgiveness for sins and eternal life through His grace, mercy, and love. Yet how many run back to thank Him? How many run to Him? How many will run to be with Him? How many will run to believe Him?

Will you be like those who ran back?

Be like the one leper out of ten who ran back to thank Jesus (Luke 17:11-19).

Be like the one woman who fell at the feet of Jesus weeping in gratitude (Luke 7:37-48).

Be like the one man who climbed a tree to see Jesus, and in gratitude changed his life (Luke 19:1-10).

Be like Joshua and Caleb who believed God was big enough to win any battle (Numbers 13:25-33, Numbers 14:1-10).

Be one in a million like Joshua who stood outside the tent, and stayed as close to God as he could (Exodus 33:11).

Be like the one who jumped out of the boat to walk on water with Jesus (Matthew 14:25-29).

Be like those who don't shrink back but will continue in faith (Hebrews 10:37-39).

Be like those who had faith to believe and trust God (Hebrews 11).

Be one who perseveres through trials and receives the crown of life (James 1:12).

Be one who will always press on to be with Jesus (Philippians 3:13-15).

Be one who will run the race to the very end (Hebrews 12:1, 1 Corinthians 9:24).

Be a runner, friends. Run to Jesus and run with Jesus to the blessings of eternal life!

Will you be one who runs back to Jesus to thank Him, adore Him, and serve Him? Will you take a moment to run and thank Jesus for all He's done in your life?

Let's run the race by fixing our eyes on Jesus and running straight to Him!

Would You be Willing?

One of my friends on social media asked what people thought about the rapture (Jesus returning for His believers). Would the rapture happen before the tribulation, during, or after? The comments were rather interesting. Several people took very firm stances. Each had their opinions on what they believed would happen to those who have a relationship with Christ during the end times.

Thinking about this, I'll pose some questions.

Would you be willing to trust in God's goodness, even if times get difficult?

Will you stand firm in your beliefs even if you are persecuted?

Would you be willing to go through a time of tribulation if it meant more people were brought to God's kingdom?

Would you be willing to be martyred to save the lost?

How far will we go, how much pain will we endure, how much suffering is worth saving a soul?

Will you be willing to give yourself to save someone else?

Some are making that choice today. Some have died for their faith. Some are being tortured for their faith. Many are being persecuted right now for their faith.

Please pray for the persecuted church, please pray for believers, please pray for those who follow Christ, and pray we will stand firm on the truth of our faith in Jesus Christ.

Heavenly Father, please help me stand firm to the end and to be willing to do whatever You call me to do.

"Greater love has no one than this, that he lay down his life for his friends." ~ John 15:13

Navigating with Love

I'm directionally challenged. If you point me in any direction, I think I'm pointing north. I'm grateful our car has a compass that tells me exactly which way I'm heading. Unfortunately, I still have trouble navigating.

I'm never lost, I just go on a variety of unexpected road trips.

The Bible is a map and compass for our daily walk. God gave us His word to read and study to find His heart. With each scripture we learn more of His character, then when life's storms buffet us the Holy Spirit will draw deep from our heart to remember God's truth and love.

Each page of the Bible is rich in past and future events, and one thing remains unchanged — God's unfailing love. The Bible is a God-breathed love letter to you from the maker of the universe. God's love letter is waiting and addressed personally to you.

The Bible is filled with love stories, tragedy, triumph, heroes and villains, poetry, prose, rescues, sinful men and women changed into mighty people of God, used in mighty ways by God. There is no book more fine, more grand, more life-changing than the Bible. The Bible is written to teach, encourage, comfort, and pour out God's love to you.

Take time to sit with God. Pour out your heart. Read His word. Listen, watch, and explore the beauty of a love relationship with The One who created love. Jesus promises, "Just as the Father has loved Me, I have also loved you; abide in My love." ~ John 15:9 (NASB)

God is your heavenly Father. When you talk to Him, He leans down from heaven to intently listen and lovingly gaze on His beloved child. God loves you and is so glad you are His! "See how great a love the Father has bestowed on us, that we would be called children of God; and such we are..." ~ 1 John 3:1 (NASB)

Regardless of where the journey of life may lead, you can be assured your Heavenly Father will provide loving navigation.

Instead Of...

Instead of fixating on the news, fix your eyes on Jesus.

Instead of reading bad news, read The Good News.

Instead of carrying a rock of anxiety, stand firm on The Rock.

Instead of looking for a word from friends, look to The Word.

Instead of pointing out the flaws of others, point to The Flawless One.

Instead of holding onto the world, hold onto The One who made the world.

Instead of spending your time on non-eternal things, spend your time with The Eternal One.

Instead of flopping around in the worries of life, flip your concerns to praise the One who is life.

Instead of shouldering your burdens, cast your burdens on the shoulder of The One who made your shoulders.

Every day we have choices to make. Instead of looking to the world, looking at our problems, and looking at other people, we can be steady by looking to God.

"The steadfast of mind You will keep in perfect peace, because he trusts in You." ~ Isaiah 26:3 (NASB)

"Give careful thought to the paths for your feet and be steadfast in all your ways." ~ Proverbs 4:26 (NIV)

"The steadfast love of the Lord never ceases; his mercies never come to an end; they are new every morning; great is your faithfulness." ~ Lamentations 3:22-23 (ESV)

Impossible to Remove?

Jesus said to them, "With people this is impossible, but with God all things are possible." ~ Matthew 19:26 (NASB)

Nothing is impossible for our God, and I think most of us can joyfully proclaim that fact. However, in the midst of difficult situations it's often hard to remember. When life is pressing down, and the finances are too small, and the bills are too big. When illness has attacked, and no cure is in sight. When love has grown cold, and our love is walking out the door. When evil is rampant, and goodness is hard to find. The problems of this world can leave us reeling and desperate for a firm footing.

To renew hope, I needed to apply God's truth. So, for each difficulty, I changed my prayers to remember that nothing is impossible for God.

Heavenly Father, the finances are so very low, help me to remember nothing is impossible for You.

Heavenly Father, the sickness isn't going away, help me to trust in You for nothing is impossible for You.

Heavenly Father, the relationship is broken and doesn't seem fixable, help me to remember nothing is impossible for You.

Heavenly Father, life can be so evil and there are everything seems so hopeless, help me to always remember You are a good God, You are always in control, and nothing is impossible for You.

Heavenly Father, remove the ache of loss, for nothing is impossible for You.

Heavenly Father, remove the fear of the past, present, or future, for nothing is impossible for You.

Heavenly Father, remove the pain of what others have done to me though their evil actions and evil words, for nothing is impossible for You.

Heavenly Father, remove the sting of betrayal, for nothing is impossible for You.

Heavenly Father, remove the worries of tomorrow, for nothing is impossible for You.

Heavenly Father, remove any negative visuals from the past and replace them with positive visuals, for nothing is impossible for You.

Heavenly Father, remove my focus on the things of this world to focus on You, for nothing is impossible for You.

Heavenly Father, remove that which hinders me from running the race You have planned for me, for nothing is impossible for You.

Heavenly Father, remove any desire that doesn't please You, for nothing is impossible for You.

Thank You, Father. I love You and praise You forever. Thank You that nothing is impossible for You.

Are you having a hard time dealing with the past, your current situation, a person or persons, or another issue? Remember nothing is impossible for God!

May I have a window seat, please?

My body does not travel well. I've been car-sick, sea-sick, air-sick, and land-sick. Movement makes me nauseous. If I'm on a boat (oh please don't put me on a boat), I have to keep my eyes focused on the horizon. If I'm in a car, I must keep looking forward.

When flying on an airplane if I don't look outside and mentally ground myself, my stomach gets queasy, and my little brain gets all discombobulated. A window seat is most important for the sake of myself and my fellow passengers, plus I want to see the journey and know where I'm going.

In the journey of life, we don't always get a window seat. We can't see beyond the moment.

God knows the future, and He never leaves us or forsakes us. In Matthew chapter six, Jesus tells us to not worry about tomorrow because our loving God knows our every need. We can't see with human eyes what's coming next, but God is already there to meet every need.

Even when we don't get a window seat, and life makes us queasy and uneasy, God's mighty hand will never let us go.

"Shouts of joy and victory resound in the tents of the righteous: 'The Lord's right hand has done mighty things!'" ~ Psalm 118:15 (NIV)

"For You have been my help, and in the shadow of Your wings I sing for joy." ~ Psalm 63:7 (NASB)

Keep Good Records

I long for God's constant guidance, a step-by-step plan for each moment of every day. However, there are times my prayers are very vague because it's easy to simply pray for God's blessings, guidance, and protection. Although those requests are good, if I don't make specific requests, I may not see how God has specifically answered.

Keeping a prayer journal has given me the ability to see how God has answered my prayers, how He has guided my steps, comforted through hard times, and worked in my life.

When I take the time to record my requests and also the answers given by God, and how He has moved, it provides hope, strength, encouragement, and joy for the journey.

Step-by-step guidance requires step-by-step requests. Asking specific requests for specific needs, helps reveal specific answers.

Will you take the time to bring specific requests to God, record them, and watch how He answers?

"In the morning, O Lord, You will hear my voice; In the morning I will order my prayer to You and eagerly watch." ~ Psalm 5:3 (NASB)

"Be anxious for nothing, but in everything by prayer and supplication with thanksgiving let your requests be made known to God." ~ Philippians 4:6 (NASB)

Travel Light

Our family visited the Oregon Trail Interpretive Center where life-sized dioramas recreate the journey of those who traveled the Oregon Trail. I'm amazed, absolutely awe-struck at those who ventured across endless, dry, hot prairie, over mountains, and treacherous rivers. The trail is marked by graves and heartache.

The numbers of travelers are estimated between 200,000 and 500,000, and ruts from wagon wheels remain in the landscape. Can you imagine traveling six months without gas stations, coffee shops, restaurants and a hotel? Plus, no facilities for us prim and proper ladies. Gasp, wheeze ...

Letters recorded what they packed often resulted in life or death. Cook stoves, silver, china, even pianos, littered the landscape as travelers left behind non-essential belongings. I don't think my cellphone or computer would have made it very far. Makes me shudder.

Thank goodness, I don't have to travel the Oregon Trail, but it sure makes me wonder–am I holding on to things that will drag me down or hinder my journey?

The writer of Hebrews tells us to "...strip off and throw aside every encumbrance (unnecessary weight) and that sin which so readily (deftly and cleverly) clings to and entangles us and let us run with patient endurance and steady and active persistence the appointed course of the race that is set before us." ~ Hebrews 12:1 (AMP)

Traveling light was essential for the success of the pioneers and also for our Christian walk. We don't need to hold on to anything holding us back from running the race God has giving us to run.

Would you be willing to pray and ask God to reveal the things you may be unnecessarily carrying on your journey?

Don't open the door

My office is where I spend most of the daytime hours. During the cold months, I close the door and turn on my little heater until the room is nice and toasty. However, if the door opens, a blast of cold air rushes in around my legs and feet.

In the same way, we've got to keep the door closed to the enemy's cold lies and distractions.

Don't open the door to worry.

Don't open the door to those thoughts that lead you on a dark path.

Don't open the door to whining and complaining.

Don't open the door to pride.

Don't open the door to lust.

Don't open the door to those who will lead you away from God.

Don't open the door to listen to the enemy lies.

Don't open the door to the many distractions to distract you from God.

Don't open the door to rehash the past over, and over, and over, and over, and over, and over again. Take the past to Jesus, who heals, restores, and redeems, over, and over, and over, and over again.

Open the door to the truth of God's Word and who you are in Christ.

Keep the door closed against the enemy and keep the door open to Jesus!

No Pout!

Ever watched a little child pout? Their bottom lip sticks out; their little face scrunches up relaying the obvious body language signs they are not happy. Not. One. Bit!

What might look cute on a small child does not look pretty on an adult. We can't always choose what happens to us, but we can choose how we will react. Every day life will hit us with reasons to pout, which also gives us opportunities to think and act in ways that honor God.

We can pout when things don't go our way, or we can remember The Way Who we follow. There is no guarantee life will always be good, yet as a Christian we are guaranteed a happy ending. Even when life is unfair and the situation seems hopeless, remember God is always just and loving.

When negative thoughts come in, take them captive, and reject any unseemly thoughts. The world sees enough negative reactions. Let's be ones who pour out God's positive, unfailing truth.

Put away the pouting and replace your mood (and your body language) with the positive, unfailing truth of God's hope, grace, mercy, and love.

Put		**Pour**
Out	and	**Out**
Unseemly		**Unfailing**
Thoughts		**Truth**

"Why are you down in the dumps, dear soul? Why are you crying the blues? Fix my eyes on God—soon I'll be praising again. He puts a smile on my face. He's my God." ~ Psalm 42:5 (MSG)

Wrap It Up!

Two o'clock in the morning and my eyes flew open. Another bad dream. Fear's heavy talons gripped my mind. Illness had left me weak and helpless, and I worried about getting older, weaker, and being alone.

In the darkness, I whispered the name – *Jesus* — The Name of my Savior and rescuer. I prayed for help.

Bible verses came to mind and light shone on God's truth. The things I was worried about I wrapped them in God's truth and the worries went away!

Even to your old age and gray hairs I am He who will sustain you. I have made you and I will carry you; I will sustain you and I will rescue you. ~ Isaiah 46:4

The LORD goes before you and will be with you; He will never leave you nor forsake you. Do not be afraid; do not be discouraged. ~ Deuteronomy 31:8

When you pass through the waters, I will be with you; and when you pass through the rivers, they will not sweep over you. When you walk through the fire, you will not be burned; the flames will not set you ablaze. ~ Isaiah 43:2

God's faithful love never ends! His mercies never cease. Great is His faithfulness; His mercies are new every morning. ~ Lamentations 3:22-23

When I am afraid, I will trust in You. ~ Psalm 56:3

The Lord is my strength and my song; He has become my salvation. He is my God, and I will praise him, my father's God, and I will exalt him. ~ Exodus 15:2

The LORD is my strength and my shield; my heart trusts in Him, and I am helped. My heart leaps for joy and I will give thanks to Him in song. ~ Psalm 28:7

Surely God is my salvation; I will trust and not be afraid. The Lord is my strength and my song; He has become my salvation. ~ Isaiah 12:2

The Sovereign Lord is my strength; He makes my feet like the feet of a deer; He enables me to go on the heights. ~ Habakkuk 3:19.

Cast your cares on the LORD and He will sustain you; He will never let the righteous fall. ~ Psalm 55:22

God will meet all your needs according to his glorious riches in Christ Jesus. ~ Philippians 4:19

When you are afraid and worried, wrap up those worries in God's truth and smother those fears and worries away.

Feeling Empty?

Ever have one of those days where you feel just totally empty? Jeremiah 2:5 tells of people who went far from God and "walked after emptiness and became empty." The people didn't pursue God and were left void of God, empty in mind, heart, body, and soul.

I wonder how much time is spent on worthless and futile pursuits? Everything on this earth is temporal. No house, job, no amount of money, can eternally fill and fulfill an empty heart. The only thing that can save a soul and fill a soul is Jesus. Jesus is the fullness who "fills all in all." ~ Ephesians 1:23

So, let's fill up with Jesus! The love of Christ surpasses knowledge and fills to "all the fullness of God." ~ Ephesians 3:19

Is your soul thirsty and hungry? Find soul-filling satisfaction in God. "Let them give thanks to the Lord for His lovingkindness, and for His wonders to the sons of men! For He has satisfied the thirsty soul, and the hungry soul He has filled with what is good." ~ Psalm 107:8-9 (NASB)

Forget the empty calories of this world. Fill your mouth with praise. "My mouth is filled with Your praise and with Your glory all day long." ~ Psalm 71:8 (NASB)

Hunger and thirst for righteousness, for that is where you find your filling. "Blessed are those who hunger and thirst for righteousness, for they will be filled." ~ Matthew 5:6 (NIV)

Let's be like the disciples who were "continually filled with joy and with the Holy Spirit." ~ Acts 13:52

No need to ever feel empty when you are in Jesus. For when you abide with Jesus, you are filled to the full and filled to the brim with His joy.

Dethatch the Thatch!

Although winter remained, sunshine beckoned. Using a small hand rake, I scratched at any matted or dead patches in our yard to remove thatch that had built up over the winter.

Even though our grass was only green in a few places, the areas now looked healthier. The thatch had kept our lawn from receiving the air, water, sunshine, and nutrients needed.

I wondered how much thatch is in my own life? What is keeping me from receiving the nutrients and sustenance needed from God and His word? Am I willing to allow God to uncover the areas that have stunted my growth?

I don't want anything to block God's Sonshine. I need to allow God to detach the thatch.

Thatch removal is not a comfortable process. Allowing God free access may be a touch painful but so worth the new life that will spring forth.

Heavenly Father, bring the spring back into my life by removing anything that blocks Your Sonshine. Detach any thatch in my life that keeps me from running free and hinders You.

Needing thatch removal? What is hindering you in your walk with God?

Let us throw off everything that hinders and the sin that so easily entangles and let us run with perseverance the race marked out for us (Hebrews 12:1).

Wanting the Best

Have you ever had a disagreement with someone, and feelings were hurt? Or perhaps a friend didn't act very friendly? Relationships are with imperfect people, and still we hope and want them to act in a perfect manner. The Lord knows sometimes people are just downright mean, gossipy, and unforgiving. Ouch!

We can't change how another person acts or reacts, but we have a choice how we act and react. We have a choice whether we will run to God or sit and stew in our hurt. We have a choice in how (and if) we will move forward. We have a choice in taking the situation (and people) to God, trusting He will do what is best and right for all concerned.

Remember God loves His children and wants the best for them — that includes the person you are having difficulties with, the person you don't like, and/or the person who you don't want to forgive, or who won't forgive you.

God wants the best for you, and He also wants their best. Regardless of the failure of others, we can pray for God's best for them because God's best is the best for us all. Keep your focus on God, trust His unfailing love, and trust that His best is the bestest for us all.

Trust God (Proverbs 3:5-6).

God will show you what is best (Isaiah 48:17).

Bless those who persecute you (Romans 12:14).

Be kind to one another, tender-hearted, forgiving, just as Christ forgave you (Ephesians 4:32).

Forgive and you will be forgiven (Matthew 6:14).

Remember you'll be judged like you judged (Matthew 7:2).

Love one another (John 13:34-35).

Don't become weary in doing good and don't give up (Galatians 6:9).

Pursue the things which make for peace and build up one another (Romans 14:19).

Encourage one another (1 Thessalonians 4:18).

Pray for one another (James 5:16).

Will you join me in praying for God's best for yourself and others?

"Now for this very reason also, applying all diligence, in your faith supply moral excellence, and in your moral excellence, knowledge, and in your knowledge, self-control, and in your self-control, perseverance, and in your perseverance, godliness, and in your godliness, brotherly kindness, and in your brotherly kindness, love." ~ 2 Peter 1:5-7 (NASB)

"Finally, brothers and sisters, rejoice! Strive for full restoration, encourage one another, be of one mind, live in peace. And the God of love and peace will be with you." ~ 2 Corinthians 13:11 (NIV)

Waiting

I wonder how much of my waiting has been because I was so busy looking for the next thing, I couldn't see the thing God was doing? In my grappling with the wait, the wait always becomes very weighty.

I've been stuck in the waiting mode far too many times. Although I have a tendency to see myself in a virtual waiting room, in fact my freedom never does hinge on a change in a situation. I am always free to love God, pray, trust Him, believe Him, and have faith in Him. The only one who boxes me in a waiting room, is me.

Waiting doesn't have to mean inactivity and frustration. Regardless of our circumstances, we are always free in Christ.

On an airplane, we may be buckled into our seats, but we are still moving through the air. Buckled into God, our lives are always in motion.

Are you in the "waiting" room? Are you frustrated at the inactivity in your situation? Please remember your soul is always unhindered and in motion in the freedom of Christ.

Let's fly while we wait! "Those who wait on the LORD shall renew their strength; they shall mount up with wings like eagles, they shall run and not be weary, they shall walk and not faint." ~ Isaiah 40:31 (NKJV)

My sweet friend, Teena Goble, filled me in on some wonderful truths about that verse. "The word 'renew' is actually the word meaning 'exchange.' Exchange means we give up something in order to get something else. So, the idea in the Hebrew is this: we give God our strength, and in exchange, He gives us His!

"The word 'wait' is the word that carries the idea of intertwining, much like what happens when we braid hair – the strands are woven together (intertwined) until they are no longer two or three separate strands, but one.

"The idea is during the waiting season, God is using that time, and that process, to intertwine our will with His, so when He is finished, and the waiting is done, there are no longer TWO wills, but ONE — His. Waiting is not a passive activity, but an active one.

"The process is so complete it carries the idea of 'intersection.' It's the place where two roads meet, and in that intersection, it's impossible to tell which road is which. It works that same way in our heart – the intertwining process is so complete, that it's impossible to tell His will from ours – they have become so perfectly One." ~ Teena Goble

I love that! In the wait, our loving Master bids us to come and abide with Him to find the joy of His presence. Intertwined in the wait, we are intertwined with our God.

Happy sigh....

Joy in the Unknown

Whatever is unknown in your life, whatever you are worried about, whatever may be ahead, you can have joy, because there is nothing unknown with God.

God loves you and knows the number of your days. He is the Alpha and the Omega, the beginning, and the end. He knows the past, present, and future because He is in the past, present, and future. God is timeless.

God knows your next steps; He knows the way you should go, and He will be with you.

God knows what you have gone through and will help you through whatever you go through. He will help you by already having the provisions in place because He knows the way and knows the plans He has for you.

God knows your thoughts and dreams. He knows what you need and will provide for every need.

God knows your sin and has enough grace to cover every sin.

God will never leave you or forsake you. He loves you. He knitted you together in your mother's womb and He will be with you all the days of your life.

Have joy, take joy, and enjoy the joy of knowing that nothing is unknown with God!

See 1 John 2:12, Hebrews 13:20-21, Isaiah 1:18, Isaiah 43:2, Jeremiah 29:11, Matthew 28:20, Philippians 4:19, Psalm 9:10, Psalm 16:11, Psalm 31:7, Psalm 37:18, Psalm 94:11, Psalm 139:1-18, Revelation 1:8

Hoping on Hope

I've prayed long and hard, and at times wondered if my prayers would make an impact. My hope runs low, but then I remember God is the God of hope.

I don't have to lose hope about a situation changing, or a person changing, because hope is found in God. God's hope is inexhaustible. God's hope never fails, and nothing is impossible for Him.

So even when my hope is so very small, I must remember, always remember, God is SO VERY BIG and He is the source of hope. If I place my hope in Him, then His hope flows back to me, and my hope grows because anything rooted in God will be sustained and continue to continue.

Heavenly Father, when my hope is low please help me remember Your ways are so very high. Your love never fails and even though a situation looks hopeless, I can find the hope needed by looking to You. Thank You I can rest in You, for all hope comes through You!

"Oh, I must find rest in God only, because my hope comes from him!" ~ Psalm 62:5 (CEB)

"I pray that God, the source of hope, will fill you completely with joy and peace because you trust in him. Then you will overflow with confident hope through the power of the Holy Spirit." ~ Romans 15:13 (NLT)

Flopping to Flipping

In the middle of the night I woke worried about an extended family member. Flopping, tossing, and turning I took my concerns to God. Or should I say I wrestled with my concerns and hoped God was listening.

Then it hit me, I needed to remember to praise. Philippians 4:6-7 tells us "Don't worry about anything; instead, pray about everything. Tell God what you need and thank him for all he has done. Then you will experience God's peace, which exceeds anything we can understand. His peace will guard your hearts and minds as you live in Christ Jesus."

I definitely needed peace, so I flipped my concerns into praises.

The prayers went from, "Help _ _ _ _ _ _ with their situation" to "Thank You Father that no situation is too big for You."

Every concern turned to a praise, and as the focus changed, the prayers became bigger, and the strength became bigger, and the comfort became bigger, and the peace became bigger, and the knowledge of God's might and power, became **bigger**.

The problems that loomed so very large at the beginning became tiny in the presence of Almighty, loving, all-magnificent, creator of the universe, nothing-is-impossible God.

Praise and thanksgiving provide soul-restoration, so flip the worries to praise and watch your concerns flop away.

The Incredible Power of Word and Tone

Two videos showed the effect of tone and words on water and salt. Sound waves changed the structure and response of the two substances. Positive spoken words formed beauty and harmony creating beautiful images similar to snowflakes. Negative words and tones created shapes of disharmony and disunity.

Imagine how words and tone affect our inner-being. I think most of us can remember hurtful words and the negative tone of others. Harmful words slice into our soul, while positive words of affirmation uplift and encourage.

Every word spoken has the power of life or death. Every word creates a reaction within ourselves and within those around us. Be very careful with your words. Be very careful what your ears hear and what you speak. Speak life. Chose words of beauty and life.

Another caution about our words is found in Matthew 12:37, Jesus said we will be justified or condemned by our words. Yikes, pass the muzzle! Be CAREFUL with your tone and words!

Start today by paying attention not only the words you speak, but the tone you use. Think, write and speak words of life and life will flow in you and out of you.

"Death and life are in the power of the tongue, and those who love it will eat its fruit." ~ Proverbs 18:21 (NASB)

Wiper Praise

My brain was worried and confused. I kept trying to analyze a situation even though I didn't really know much about the situation. My thoughts were spinning in the mud and not going anywhere, so I decided to sing praise songs and get my mind off my problems and back on God.

And the coolest thing happened, as I sang praise songs and praised God, the confusion lifted, and I was given clarity. Peace and answers came, and joy followed. So, I praised all the more, and enjoyed more peace, clarity, and joy.

I've decided praise is like a mind windshield wiper. Praise wipes away confusion to see things clearly through God's perspective.

When your brain is muddied and confused with worries, activate praising God for clarity, peace, and joy.

"He is your praise, and He is your God, who has done for you these great and awesome things which your eyes have seen." ~ Deuteronomy 10:21 (NKJV)

"Rejoice in the Lord, O you righteous! For praise from the upright is beautiful." ~ Psalm 33:1 (NKJV)

"My lips will shout for joy when I sing praises to You; and my soul, which You have redeemed." ~ Psalm 71:23 (NASB)

"Shout joyfully to the Lord, all the earth; break forth and sing for joy and sing praises." ~ Psalm 98:4 (NASB)

The Key to a Delightful Life

While Reading through Deuteronomy, I noticed the blessings God pronounced over the Israelites if they would follow and obey Him.

The key to life is found in loving and obeying God. "...**choose life**, so that you and your descendants might live! You can **make this choice by loving the Lord your God, obeying him, and committing yourself firmly to him. This is the_ key to your life**." ~ Deuteronomy 30:19-20a (NLT)

God's delights come through obedience. "**The Lord your God will delight in you if you obey his voice and keep the commands** and decrees written in this Book of Instruction, and if you turn to the Lord your God with all your heart and soul." ~ Deuteronomy 30:10 (NLT)

Joy is found in the seeking of God, the seeking of His will, and the seeking of His presence. "**May all who search for you be filled with joy and gladness in you**..." ~ Psalm 40:16 (NLT) "You will make known to me the path of life; **in Your presence is fullness of joy;** in Your right hand there are pleasures forever." ~ Psalm 16:11 (NASB)

In trusting God, we find His help and joy. "The Lord is my strength and my shield; **my heart trusted in Him, and I am helped; therefore my heart greatly rejoices**, and with my song I will praise Him." ~ Psalm 28:7 (NKJV)

Want to really live life? "You shall **love the Lord your God with all your heart, and with all your soul, and with all your strength, and with all your mind; and your neighbor as yourself ... do this and you will live**." ~ Luke 10:27-28 (NASB)

Unlock joy by trusting, obeying, and serving God. "**Serve the Lord with gladness**; come before His presence with singing." ~ Psalm 100:2 (NKJV) "Trust in the Lord, and do good; dwell in the land, and feed on His faithfulness. **Delight yourself also in the Lord**, and He shall give you the desires of your heart." ~ Psalm 37:3-4 (NKJV) **Love the Lord, follow and obey Him, and find a joyful and delightful life!** (Bold and underline mine)

Keep Praying

Pray -- Keep praying.
   Be persistent. Keep knocking. Keep seeking the Lord.

Keep praying for your brothers and sisters in Christ.
   Pray they seek the Lord in all things.
   Pray they keep their lives and homes free from the stain of sin.
   Pray they read God's word and know God's word.
   Pray they will be bold in love to show and tell others of Christ.

Keep praying for the persecuted church.
   Pray they will stand firm.
   Pray they will know God is with them.
   Pray they will experience God's comfort, peace, and
   strength even in their difficult circumstances.

Keep praying for the lost.
   Pray that their blind eyes are opened.
   Pray that their stone hearts are melted to receive Jesus.

Keep praying for those in leadership to seek God's face.
Keep praying for your family.
Keep praying for your pastor.
Keep praying for those in ministry.
Keep praying for those who are caregivers.
Keep praying for the workers who work so very hard.
Keep praying for those who are single.
Keep praying for widows and widower.
Keep praying for single moms and dads.
Keep praying for married couples.
Keep praying for students.
Keep praying for teachers.
Keep praying for your neighbors.
Keep praying for you to have God's heart to know how to pray.
Keep praying, for your prayers matter for now and eternity.

Keep praying, for your prayers block the enemy, defeat.
strongholds, and set captives free.
Keep praying for God's kingdom come, His will be done,
on earth as it is in heaven.
Keep praying, keep praying, keep praying!

Please take a moment right now to pray.

In the Silence

There are days I'm desperate, so very desperate for God's presence. My soul is parched, weary, and my hands reach out and so long for the touch of heaven's love.

And all seems silent.

I cry, beg, and plead. I pray, "I need You God. I need You!"

And all seems silent.

I check and double-check to make sure sin isn't blocking. I check to see if there is something I haven't done I should have done. Or something I shouldn't have done that I did. I read God's word, pray, beg, and plead more.

And all seems silent.

I wonder if God is ever-present, why can't I feel His presence?

In the silence, I chose to believe.

In the silence, I chose to praise.

God I can't feel You right now, but I believe You are here. I believe You are with me. I believe You love me. Thank You that You are here. Thank You for Your love. Thank You for who You are. Thank You for all You do. Thank You for loving me. Thank You for Your unfailing love. Thank You that You will supply all I need. Thank You that You are the answer to everything I need. Thank You that even in my flailing, whining, searching, and begging, You still love me.

And in the silence, peace comes.

In the silence, love falls fresh.

In the silence, I believe.

In the silence, He is here.

"My soul waits in silence for God only; from Him is my salvation. My soul, wait in silence for God only, for my hope is from Him." ~ Psalm 62:1, Psalm 62:5 (NASB)

Kneel Power

The list for my day is long and scattered in different directions. Errands need to be run, work needs to be completed, and I'm not even sure where to start.

I hit the ground running, but it feels I'm only running in circles.

Then a gentle reminder comes to kneel to find the time and wisdom to complete each task.

Instead of hitting the ground running, I need to remember to hit the ground kneeling.

Kneeling is the power plug to plug into The Power of God.

Is your list long and scattered? Kneel power gives God power!

"Come, let us worship and bow down, let us kneel before the Lord our Maker." ~ Psalm 95:6 (NASB)

The Secret to Trust

Ever wrestled with trusting God? I'll be honest, I have! So, I asked God, "What is Trust? How can I trust?"

My first stop was the Webster's 1828 Dictionary to understand better the definition of the word "Trust" (The 1828 dictionary doesn't just give the definitions but also Bible verses.)

Here's what I found. TRUST is confidence; a reliance or resting of the mind on the integrity, veracity, justice, friendship or other sound principle of another person. Trust is something committed to a person's care for use or management, and for which an account must be rendered. Confidence; special reliance on supposed honesty.

As I pondered these truths, this verse came to mind, "<u>Trust</u> in the Lord <u>with all your heart</u> and lean not on your own understanding. <u>In all your ways</u> acknowledge Him, and He will direct your paths" ~ Proverbs 3:5-6 (NASB) (underline mine).

Using blueletterbible.org, I checked the original Hebrew for the underlined words listed in the verse above. These words stood out from the definitions I found -- reliance or resting of the mind, bold, courageous in every part of the journey.

Father I want to trust You (be reliant on You with the resting of my mind, bold and courageous) with all my heart. How can I do this, Father? Lord, I believe, help my unbelief. Lord, I trust, help my untrust.

Again, the verse came, "Trust in the Lord with all your heart and lean not on your own understanding. In all your ways acknowledge Him, and He will direct your paths." ~ Proverbs 3:5-6

This time <u>acknowledge Him</u> stood out. which means to know, learn to know. Therefore, bold, courageous, resting in God trust, comes from knowing Him and acknowledging Him in all things.

Trust comes from shining the light on any unrest with the knowledge of who God is, with the knowledge and revelation of our great God.

The God who created the universe, who can do all things. The God of everything and everyone, not bound by space or time.

The God who loves with an unfailing love. The God who will direct my path, no matter where the journey, direction, or road leads.

Trust comes from remembering God, remembering His promises, remembering His provision, remembering (causing to know!) God! To know God is to trust Him! To Trust Him is to know Him!

When we trust God, we remain in the state of **confident trust** because we know Who is our Trust.

The more we dig into the Bible and find the deeper meanings, the more we can apply God's truth to our lives. What words and verses help you trust in our amazing trustworthy God?

Battling

Dear battling friend,

...battling in the heavenlies for yourself and/or loved ones.
...battling through loneliness.
...battling depression.
...battling the medical diagnosis.
...battling sleeplessness.
...battling worries and concerns.
...battling to understand.
...battling to love the unlovely.
...battling pain.
...battling to know what to do next.
...battling for your marriage.
...battling for a job, an open door, a word from heaven.
...battling and so very tired of being in the battle.
...battling just plain battling to stand on your faith.
...battling when the answers haven't come.

The enemy wants you to give up, throw down your sword, and walk away. Don't do it!

Keep battling, keep praying, keep trusting and believing, even when your trust and belief seems so very small. Faith the size of a mustard seed moves mountains.

Even when we can't find faith, God is faithful. Even tiny prayers make huge impacts because our God is a HUGE God.

With God comes victory, answers, positive change, relief, compassion, wisdom, comfort, rest, unfailing love, protection, grace, mercy, defense, courage, strength, and joy. Keep fighting, hold on to God even when you can't stand and can't seem to find the handhold. In every battle there is a victor, and if you are in Christ, you **will** always have victory.

Heavenly Father, the battle is so very long, so very hard, and my strength is so very small. Please help me and my friends who are battling. We need You! Thank You that in Your Son, Jesus Christ, we have victory to overcome any battle we face. Father, I humbly ask for Your help for my brothers and sisters in the midst of their battles. Please surround them with Your strength and unfailing love.

Father, thank You even when we are weak, You are strong. Thank You that You never leave us or forsake us. Thank You that You are mighty and all-powerful, and nothing is too hard for You. Thank You nothing is impossible for You. We are tired, we are weary, and we are bloody from the battle, but we will rest in the shadow of Your wings.

We love You Father, and we ask these things in the name of Your Son, Jesus Christ who is our Savior. Amen.

Look at Me

I kept thinking about a situation, and the more I thought about that situation, the more upsetting it became.

Then I felt a gentle whisper in my soul, "*Look at Me.*" As I turned my gaze on the Lord, peace came.

Unfortunately, being one who thinks I can figure out something if I'll just keep trying to analyze it, I kept taking my eyes off of Jesus and back on the difficulty. I'm like Peter sinking in the waves instead of walking on water. Again, the gentle whisper came, "*Look at Me.*" I sensed no condemnation. No anger. I turned back to look, and peace came.

Being the stubborn type, I took my eyes off Jesus and waves of anxiety washed over me. "*Look at Me.*" He beckoned.

This time I locked on His gaze, and as my focus stayed on God, the more He grew, and in the shadow of His love, the situation faded in the light of His glory.

Look at Me. Keep your focus on Me. Not on them. Not on that person. Not on that situation.

Keep your focus on Me. Not on that concern. Not on that possibility. Not on that worry.

Keep your focus on Me. Not on the news. Not on the violence. Not on those who hate.

Keep your focus on Me. Not on the unknown. Not on the future. Not on the past.

Keep your focus on Me. Not on the waves. Not on the wind. Not on the storm.

Keep your focus on Me. And watch how I will work. And see what I will do. And rest in My love.

Keep your focus on Me. Remember, nothing is impossible for Me. Remember, I know the plans I have for you. Remember, I can melt stone hearts.

Keep your focus on Me. Remember, I know the truth and will judge righteously. Remember, I Am the God of comfort. Remember, I Am the God of peace.

Keep your focus on Me. When the waves of anxiety come, remember to always keep your focus on Me. Remember, I will never leave you. Remember, I will never forsake you. Remember, always I love you.

Keep your focus on Me.

"Keep your eyes on Jesus, who both began and finished this race we're in. Study how he did it. Because he never lost sight of where he was headed—that exhilarating finish in and with God—he could put up with anything along the way: Cross, shame, whatever. And now he's there, in the place of honor, right alongside God. When you find yourselves flagging in your faith, go over that story again, item by item, that long litany of hostility he plowed through. That will shoot adrenaline into your souls!" ~ Hebrews 12:2 (MSG)

Courage and Comfort

Are you struggling with a difficulty?

Plug in whatever you are facing and let God's word speak to you.

Be strong and courageous. Do not be afraid or terrified because of _____, for the LORD your God goes with you; he will never leave you nor forsake you. Do not be afraid; do not be discouraged.

No one, no thing, not even _____, will be able to stand up against you all the days of your life. As I was with Moses, so I will be with you; I will never leave you nor forsake you.

So do not fear, for I am with you; do not be dismayed, for I am your God. I will strengthen you and help you; I will uphold you with my righteous right hand.

Know that the LORD has set apart the godly for himself; the LORD will hear when I call to him.

There is no health in my body. I am feeble and utterly crushed; I groan in anguish of heart. All my longings lie open before you, O Lord; my sighing is not hidden from you. My heart pounds, my strength fails me; even the light has gone from my eyes. Be merciful to me, LORD, for I am faint; O LORD, heal me, for my bones are in agony.

I am in pain and distress; may your salvation, O God, protect me.

Heal me, O LORD, and I will be healed; save me and I will be saved, for you are the one I praise.

The Spirit of the Lord GOD is upon me, because the LORD has anointed me to bring good news to the afflicted; He has sent me to bind up the brokenhearted, to proclaim liberty to captives and freedom to prisoners.

Plug in your name to make these verses personal...

The LORD will sustain _ _ _ _ _ _ _ on their sickbed and restore them from the bed of illness.

But those who suffer He delivers in their suffering; He speaks to them in their affliction.

For He has not despised or disdained the suffering of the afflicted one; He has not hidden His face from _ _ _ _ _ _ _ _ _ _ _ _ but has listened to their cry for help. _ _ _ _ _ _ _ _ _ _ _ _ _, come to Me, when you are weary and heavy-laden, and I will give you rest.

Peace I leave with you; my peace I give you. I do not give to you as the world gives. Do not let your hearts be troubled and do not be afraid.

(Deuteronomy 31:6,8, Joshua 1:5, Isaiah 41:10, Psalm 4:3, Psalm 38:7-10, Psalm 6:2, Psalm 69:29, Jeremiah 17:14, Isaiah 61:1, Psalm 41:3, Job 36:15, Psalm 22:24, Matthew 11:28, John 14:27)

Lifelines

God is a tender God who will help us through the hurts of life, illness, suffering, and the evil of people. I've always appreciated the verse in Isaiah, "When you pass through the waters, I will be with you. When you cross rivers, you will not drown. When you walk through fire, you will not be burned, nor will the flames hurt you." ~ Isaiah 43:2 (NCV)

The verse doesn't say we won't go through deep waters or encounter fiery trials, but it does promise God will be with us as we go through whatever we go through.

Looking back, I can see God's lifelines. The encouraging letter that came in the mail when I was a lonely little girl. The friends who rallied to help when I was sick. The email waiting in my inbox when I didn't think anyone cared.

God's lifelines may not be big and might not even be noticeable at the time. Through hardship and pain, God's tender touch is always there to help, perhaps through the hug of a friend, the smile of a stranger, or through God's beautiful creation.

How many times have you talked to someone who said, "I wouldn't have made it through if it hadn't been for..." and they list a person, some kind of provision, or something they saw or experienced. Something helped them make it through. That "thing" wasn't just luck. James 1:17 tells us that every good thing given, and every perfect gift is from above. Those good things came from God.

It's not just luck you've made it through your life. If you're reading this, you're a survivor. You're still here, still breathing, and still overcoming.

Whether you've seen God's hand or not, He has helped you through whatever you've been through, and He will be with you whatever comes next. God's lifelines are always there.

"We who have run for our very lives to God have every reason to grab the promised hope with both hands and never let go. It's an unbreakable spiritual lifeline, reaching past all appearances right to the very presence of God where Jesus, running on ahead of us, has taken up his permanent post as high priest for us..." ~ Hebrews 6:18-20 (MSG)

Equipped

Do you ever feel ill-equipped to handle the circumstances or people in your life? Do you wonder if you'll make it through the next trial or difficulty?

I have good news, very good news! If you are a Jesus follower, whatever has happened in your life, whatever you face, God has equipped you. You are never without what is needed to recover and move forward. Since God is here in the now, and He is already in the future, He will be with you on every step of your journey.

The phone call that rocked your world, the flood that washed away your home, the destroying fire, the pain of the past, and the suffering of the future, nothing is too much for God. Nothing catches Him by surprise, and nothing will come that God has not already equipped you to go through. The same is for those you love or those who you hear about on the news. Whatever happens in their life, whatever they face, God has equipped them.

The Greek definition of equipping is, to be complete, furnishing, perfecting. Equipping is a mending, arranging, adjusting, strengthening, completing to be perfected through the all-encompassing power of Jesus Christ. Equipping is sufficiency to be sufficient through God.

I picture each of us born with a virtual backpack of God-goodies for our life journey. Every provision is already in place for our every need because God already knows the needs we'll have for each day.

Rest content friends, you are equipped!

"Jesus has the power of God, by which he has given us everything we need to live and to serve God. We have these things because we know him. Jesus called us by his glory and goodness. Through these he gave us the very great and precious promises. With these gifts you can share in God's nature." ~ 2 Peter 1:3-4a (NCV)

"Now the God of peace, who brought up from the dead the great Shepherd of the sheep through the blood of the eternal covenant, even Jesus our Lord, equip you in every good thing to do His will, working in us that which is pleasing in His sight, through Jesus Christ, to whom be the glory forever and ever. Amen." ~ Hebrews 13:20-21 (NASB)

"Do not be anxious about anything, but in every situation, by prayer and petition, with thanksgiving, present your requests to God." ~ Philippians 4:6 (NIV)

"All Scripture is inspired by God and profitable for teaching, for reproof, for correction, for training in righteousness; so that the man of God may be adequate, equipped for every good work." ~ 2 Timothy 3:16-17 (NASB)

"And He gave some as apostles, and some as prophets, and some as evangelists, and some as pastors and teachers, for the equipping of the saints for the work of service, to the building up of the body of Christ; until we all attain to the unity of the faith, and of the knowledge of the Son of God, to a mature man, to the measure of the stature which belongs to the fullness of Christ." ~ Ephesians 4:11-13 (NASB)

"His divine power has given us <u>everything we need</u> for a godly life through our knowledge of him who called us by his own glory and goodness" ~ 2 Peter 1:3 (NIV) (underline mine).

Description

How would you describe yourself?

Based on your own words, where would we find you listed in the dictionary?

I am depressed.
I am angry.
I am a victim.
I am lonely.
I am sick.
I am _____

The list goes on and on as we identify ourselves with our past, current circumstances, or feelings.

You are you. You aren't a feeling. You aren't your past. You aren't a circumstance.

You are created by the God of the Universe -- The Great "I Am." And as a believer in Jesus Christ, your identity, your true identity, is found in Him.

Remember who you are in Christ. Be careful with your words for yourself and others.

Regardless of what you have done, regardless of what has been done to you, your true identity is found in Christ. In light of that truth, who do you say you are?

Heavenly Father, help me to always remember I am Your child, and my true identity is found in the beauty of Your love. In Christ, I am forgiven, restored, redeemed, and forever loved.

Gifted

Don't you love getting gifts? Especially a gift you've always wanted.

In Matthew 25, Jesus relates the story about the wealthy owner who was going on a trip and gave his servants talents.

You too are gifted, you are given talents, you have a purpose and a place on this planet. John 1:16 and Romans 12:6 tells us we all have received one gift after another, different gifts according to the grace given to each of us. Our God-given gifts don't wear out or expire and they don't have a retirement date.

For the gifts and the calling of God are irrevocable (Romans 11:29). What we are given remains with us to be used to glorify God now and for eternity.

Mary Southerland is a speaker and writer with Girlfriends in God. When Mary's son was younger, she received a call to come talk by her son's preschool teacher. Jared was only four. Her adopted son told all his classmates he was chosen but their parents were stuck with them. Whether you were adopted or not, you were chosen by God to be born and here for such a time as this.

You are gifted, talented, and chosen.

As Christians are called the Bride of Christ. Not just subjects, servants, or even just friends, we are in an intimate relationship with God through Christ.

As a Christian, you are made for an intimate love relationship with the Creator of the Universe. You were made by joy for joy. Not just a little joy, but full abundant joy! You are a joyful gift to the world!

Replace the Bad Filter

During my teenage years we lived in an old farmhouse. Our water supply came from a well far beyond its prime. The rusty water made it difficult to drink, as well as keep clothing, sinks, and the bathtub clean. Replacing the filter on the well helped, but only for a short time. Sediment and rust would quickly overwhelm the system. The battle continued until my parents had enough money to dig a new, deeper, well to reach a clean and clear supply of water.

Society filters through a worldview tainted by the enemy's lies, clogged by anger, self-righteousness, pride, self-justification, personal agendas, and greed. Obstructions in our lives can be in place from early childhood by family, friends, and what others believe, whisper, scream, or pronounce. Regardless of what the world and society think, says, or does, the only way to find the pure Truth is in the truth of God's word.

Regardless of how messy your past, how messy your current situation, how overwhelming life may seem, God's clean, clear, truth filters away the rust and sediment of the enemy's lies.

Regardless of what others have said about you, pronounced about you, did to you, spoke over you ... God's truth is you are God's beloved child, and He loves you.

True freedom exists in God's truth, in the reality of who you are in Christ. Check your filter. Daily. Moment-by-moment. Your thoughts are under attack, your perception of yourself and others are under attack.

Check, check, and double-check to make sure what you believe and what you know about yourself, and others are filtered through God's truth, and the truth will set you free.

"You will know the truth, and the truth will make you free." John 8:32

Unmuzzle the Mouth

I've had friends with sinful pasts who feel they have no right to tell their children or others the correct way to live. Some grew up one way and were so desperate not to have their children live under the same rules and regulations, they allowed their children to do anything and everything.

Please, please, please don't allow the enemy to cause you to go to extremes or silence you. If you had a sinful past, you don't have to share the gory details, but you can share the negatives and the pitfalls because of those sins. Tell your children and tell others of God's grace but warn them of the consequences. Don't allow the enemy to silence the knowledge God has gifted you with to share with others.

Don't be so desperate to raise your children in a different way that you miss the ways God says to raise your children. Tell them of God's love. Find a good church home for you and your children where God's word is taught. Read your Bible to them and share the beauty of God's word.

You are never disqualified from advising others of the beauty of God's love, the beauty of His grace and mercy, and the beauty of new opportunities to live for Him.

Don't allow the enemy to silence you or say you are disqualified because of your failures. You are qualified to speak truth into the lives of others. Be honest about your struggles and failures (with Godly discretion) to point to the honest and unfailing, perfect love of God.

Unmuzzle the mouth to teach, speak, encourage, comfort, guide, and to tell about our wonderful God!

Do you ever hesitate to talk to your children or someone else because of your own failures? The enemy is always looking for opportunities to keep those who love God silent.

Would you please take a moment to ask God to reveal any area where you have kept silent instead of speaking truth into the lives of your children, friends, or family?

Heavenly Father, please reveal Your truth in our lives so that we can speak Your truth into the lives of those we know and love.

"You shall love the Lord your God with all your heart and with all your soul and with all your might. You shall teach them diligently to your sons and shall talk of them when you sit in your house and when you walk by the way and when you lie down and when you rise up." ~ Deuteronomy 6:5-7 (NASB)

Storm Sprouting

Something interesting happened with our bird feeder. We had several wild storms, and the rain penetrated the lower section. Because of the moisture, the sunflower seeds actually sprouted.

Storms can be frightening and unsettling, however storms bring blessings. As lightning crashes, nitrogen is released into the air which fertilizes the earth. Rain brings life-giving sustenance. And thunder ... well it creates incredible sound effects.

James tells us to consider it all joy when we encounter the storms of life, because storms/trials produce a perfect, spiritual harvest.

I don't enjoy life-storms. However, knowing something good will come, because something good always comes for God's children, I can rest in God's arms trusting that new life will sprout from each hardship.

Heavenly Father storms are scary, so please help me remember Your sustaining, nourishing power always sprouts a wonderful new life.

"Consider it all joy, my brethren, when you encounter various trials, knowing that the testing of your faith produces endurance. And let endurance have its perfect result, so that you may be perfect and complete, lacking in nothing." ~ James 1:2-4 (NASB)

No GAC

"Do everything without grumbling or arguing." ~ Philippians 2:14

Oh my, Philippians 2:14 caught my attention. Seriously? Do **Everything** without grumbling or arguing? Surely Paul didn't mean everything. So, I dug into the original Greek text and checked other Bible versions and found out the verse involves even more.

The meaning is to do all things (everything) without grumbling, complaining, murmuring, arguing, having disputes, questioning, muttering, having a secret debate, a secret displeasure not openly avowed, hesitation, doubting, disputing, and arguing.

Oh my, that seems really hard. But the amazing thing about the verse is that it was written by a man chained in prison. He even tells us to rejoice in the Lord always; and again, he says rejoice (Philippians 4:4). So, if Paul can do those things, it means I also can do everything without grumbling or complaining.

That means NO **G**rumbling **A**nd **C**omplaining – no GAC!

I guess that means we need to ...

Drive without grumbling or complaining.

Stand (or sit in your car) in a long line without grumbling or complaining.

Work in the office, or at home, without grumbling or complaining.

Meet the needs of your manager, family, children ... without grumbling or complaining.

Attend church without grumbling or complaining.

Clean house, toilets, desks ... without grumbling or complaining.

Cook meals without grumbling or complaining.

Pay bills without grumbling or complaining.

Be a caregiver, an employee, a mom, a wife, a dad, a husband, a child, a single person, a married person, a young person, an old person, an anybody person ... without grumbling or complaining.

Do anything and everything without **g**rumbling or **c**omplaining. Kick out the grumbling and complaining and you'll be amazed how your spirit will lift. And those around you will also be very grateful!

Let's shine our lights for Christ with our words, thoughts, and actions!

Heavenly Father, please guard my tongue and my thoughts to keep away the grumbling and complaining. Tender my heart to Yours to remind me always to be grateful in anything and everything I do.

I love You, Father!

"Do all things without grumbling and faultfinding and complaining [against God] and questioning and doubting [among yourselves], that you may show yourselves to be blameless and guileless, innocent and uncontaminated, children of God without blemish (faultless, unrebukable) in the midst of a crooked and wicked generation [spiritually perverted and perverse], among whom you are seen as bright lights (stars or beacons shining out clearly) in the [dark] world." ~ Philippians 2:14-15 (AMP)

Uncharted

Our son, Scott was given the opportunity to study in Japan for a college course. Once he knew where he would stay, he used Google Maps to "walk" the streets. He could "see" his location and how to get back and forth to the University where he would study.

Before Scott even went to Tokyo, he had a good idea how to travel in the city and access the train system. Once he arrived, many of the roads were familiar, and he navigated with ease. When he returned, he again used the online map system to show us where he went and the many miles he walked each day.

In the same way, God has not left us on planet earth without help and direction. The Bible is our road map. "Your word is a lamp for my feet, a light on my path" ~ Psalm 119:105 (NIV).

When we read God's word, we are given clarity and guidance, and then the Holy Spirit reminds us of God's word. We don't have to grope around in the darkness, Jesus is the light of the world, and He is the Way to show us the way. No path is uncharted for our awesome all-knowing, all-seeing God.

Joyful Heartbeats

Gratitude changes everything. If we're grateful, what we have becomes clear and what we don't have fades away. Eve had paradise, yet if she had been living in gratitude would she have even noticed the fruit? Gratitude focuses on blessings, not on lack.

Paul learned to be content, he wrote to be thankful in all circumstances. For a man who had been beaten numerous times, stoned and left for dead, ship-wrecked, imprisoned, and suffered many hardships, he still knew the secret of a thankful heart.

Thanksgiving brings freedom to enjoy life, freedom to live above and beyond our circumstances, and freedom to live in the light of God's unfailing love.

A heart of gratitude beats with joy.

A thankful heart beats with freedom to truly live.

A mind focused on Jesus lives in peace.

A life with praise and thanksgiving is a life lived well for eternity.

Let's live in gratitude so we may peacefully and joyfully live!

"In everything give thanks; for this is the will of God in Christ Jesus for you." ~ 1 Thessalonians 5:18 (NKJV)

"Be anxious for nothing, but in everything by prayer and supplication with thanksgiving let your requests be made known to God. And the peace of God, which surpasses all comprehension, will guard your hearts and your minds in Christ Jesus." ~ Philippians 4:6-7 (NASB)

Little Words

The other night my head throbbed with pain. A muscle in my neck will occasionally tighten which feels like someone has jabbed a spike in the back of my head. Ouch!

Tossing and turning during the night I hoped sleep would relax the muscles. By morning, my neck was feeling much better. Yet when my husband asked how I was, I responded I was doing a "little" better.

Little? I immediately felt a pain of guilt. I had minimized the truth. I asked the Lord for forgiveness and spoke truth to my husband that I was much better.

Then I wondered, what if the words I said, came true? What if the words spoken resulted in action? What if my body heard the word "little" and decided to only have a little healing? Ack! Goodness, I don't want just a little healing. And I sure don't want any little word to result in big consequences.

Our words contain life or death. And every word spoken results in an action internally and externally. What if our words are what hinders us?

How many times have you heard ...?

I'm doing a little better.

I'm feeling a little better.

We are financially doing a little better.

The jobs a little better.

The situations a little better.

My health is a little better.

The _____ is a little better.

Perhaps those words were true, but what if the words were spoken to minimize the situation, or to gain sympathy, or because of doubt? And as a result of those little words we minimized what God had done in our lives.

What if we took a moment before we spoke words, to make sure our words are completely true? What if we fully believed, trusted, and spoke words to make sure we are never hindered in our walk with the Lord or with others?

Let's live large in the truth by not allowing any little thing (in word or deed) to hinder our walk with God. Let's make sure our words speak truth to ourselves and others, for our little words have big consequences.

"Let the words of my mouth and the meditation of my heart be acceptable in Your sight, O Lord, my strength and my Redeemer." ~ Psalm 19:14 (NKJV)

"Pleasant words are like a honeycomb, sweetness to the soul and health to the bones." ~ Proverbs 16:24 (NKJV)

"For by your words you will be justified, and by your words you will be condemned." ~ Matthew 12:37 (NKJV)

He knows how you feel.

One of the beautiful blessings of Christianity is when we ask Jesus into our hearts, He lives in our hearts (John 15). We are given a wonderful blessing of an intimate relationship.

As I pondered this, I realized whatever I'm feeling (and facing), Jesus understands. He understands not only because He walked this earth and knows the pains and trials of humanity, but also because He lives within us. Jesus intimately understands our emotions because He is intimately living within us.

So, when you are lonely, He knows how you feel because He is there within you. When you are hurt, He knows how you feel. His sympathy goes beyond just head knowledge; He has heart knowledge because His tender heart beats within your tender heart.

Jesus truly knows how you feel. Whatever you are feeling, whatever you are facing, you are not alone. Jesus is with you, and He truly knows how you feel.

"For we do not have a high priest who cannot sympathize with our weaknesses, but One who has been tempted in all things as we are, yet without sin." ~ Hebrews 4:15 (NASB)

Lions and bears... oh my.

David was just a kid when he fought and killed a lion and a bear. He wasn't the tallest or strongest, but he believed in the power of God. He didn't whine about his battles; he celebrated the victories and thus was able to take on a giant (see 1 Samuel 17).

I wonder if we aren't conquering giants because we've forgotten to look from the proper perspective. We can whine about our battles or look to the One who helps us get through the battles.

Men didn't become knights without proof of bravery, and that proof came through combat. Fair maidens sometimes have fought the biggest battles -- the battles behind the scenes, the battles on the knees, the battles to just get through the day.

You've fought your lions and bears, and even though you have wounds, even though the battle was horrible, you fought. You survived even though you thought you wouldn't, even though you didn't think you could. If you're reading this, you are a fighter and a survivor. You don't have to be strong to win battles, as God's child you have the power of God. Lions and bears may attack but The Lion of Judah is on your side.

Let's celebrate being survivors instead of being victims. Let's celebrate making it through another battle and another day. Let's celebrate the victories we have through God!

"Thanks be to God, who gives us the victory through our Lord Jesus Christ. For whatever is born of God overcomes the world; and this is the victory that has overcome the world—our faith." 1 Corinthians 15:57 (NASB), 1 John 5:4 (NASB)

Standing

There's a story about a little boy who would not mind his parents and sit down. When they finally got the boy to sit, he replied "I may be sitting on the outside, but I'm still standing on the inside."

The little guy was stubborn and not obedient, but I want to look at that story from a different perspective. The enemy wants us as Christians to sit, be quiet, and not have a successful faith life.

However, the only thing that can hinder you, is *you.* Your inner person is never hindered. Your soul can always stand. Regardless of your circumstances, your past, your current life, who you live with, work with, or where you live, you are unhindered in Christ.

Stand for Christ even if you can't walk. Stand in the reality your life is free in Christ.

Stand in awe of God. Stand firm knowing God will guide you. Stand in the rest of God. Stand in the freedom of Christ. Stand firm in the knowledge you are loved by God with an unfailing love.

Stand, sit, kneel, and/or walk in prayer. Stand in praise. Stand firm against the enemy. Stand strong. Stand firm in God's truth. Stand firm in your faith. Always keep your soul standing firm in Christ.

Remember, "It was for freedom that Christ set us free; therefore, **keep standing firm** ..." ~ Galatians 5:1 (NASB)

Turn Back

I was so saddened when I read in Jeremiah 2 of those who turned away and chose sin instead of following after God. They walked after emptiness and became empty. "For my people have done two evil things: They have abandoned Me--the fountain of living water. And they have dug for themselves cracked cisterns that can hold no water at all!" (Jeremiah 2:5, 2:13)

We're not talking about a little slip up here and there, but a daily choice to follow after their own desires and to live a life of sin. They made their choices, willingly, and deliberately to turn from God, and judgment came.

We all have sinned and fallen short of the glory of God, yet God showed His great love for us by sending Christ to die for us while we were still sinners (Romans 3:23, Romans 5:8).

To continue in sin – willingly, knowingly, and deliberately -- is a slap in the face of grace.

Don't wink at sin, don't continue down a path you know is wrong, and don't think God won't notice or consequences won't come. Sin always has consequences, and those consequences ripple out from your sin. "Woe to those who call evil good, and good evil; who substitute darkness for light and light for darkness; who substitute bitter for sweet and sweet for bitter!" ~ Isaiah 5:20 (NASB)

Sin keeps us from God's presence.

Sin keeps us from God's best.

Sin brings destruction of relationships with God and with others.

Sin is dark and bitter.

Sin promises fulfillment, but only brings emptiness and sorrow.

Sin leads to destruction.

If sin is in your life, don't wait another moment or another day, right now, ask for God's forgiveness, turn away from that which binds you and leaves you empty.

Turn back and you'll find God's grace waiting, and in God's presence you'll find forgiveness, new mercies, fullness of joy, and freedom.

Please turn back.

"So repent [change your inner self—your old way of thinking, regret past sins] and return [to God—seek His purpose for your life], so that your sins may be wiped away [blotted out, completely erased], so that times of refreshing may come from the presence of the Lord [restoring you like a cool wind on a hot day]." ~ Acts 3:19 (AMP)

Forever Filled

Winter was coming and we drove by the Lucky Peak Reservoir near Boise, Idaho. Boaters had used the reservoir throughout the summer months, but now in preparation of the winter snow, the water level had been adjusted.

The land once covered by water was bare, and the result was both beautiful and alarming. Good thing they didn't ask me how much water to let out. I would have been stingy, hording, and worrying there wouldn't be enough for the next hot summer.

I realized I had been hording worries and not keeping my focus on God and His provision. I need to remember our vast, awesome, wonderful, loving Creator God always has and always will provide for every need. No worries are needed; no hoarding is required, because God's reservoirs are always forever filled.

"For this reason I bow my knees before the Father, from whom every family in heaven and on earth derives its name, that He would grant you, according to the riches of His glory, to be strengthened with power through His Spirit in the inner man, so that Christ may dwell in your hearts through faith; and that you, being rooted and grounded in love, may be able to comprehend with all the saints what is the breadth and length and height and depth, and to know the love of Christ which surpasses knowledge, that you may be filled up to all the fullness of God. Now to Him who is able to do far more abundantly beyond all that we ask or think, according to the power that works within us, to Him be the glory in the church and in Christ Jesus to all generations forever and ever. Amen." ~ Ephesians 3:14-21 (NASB)

Prayer hug

I love a good hug from friends or family. There's something beautifully sweet when someone you love puts their arms around you. The human touch when properly used is a blessing.

Whether someone is a hugger or not, there is one thing you can do that will bless the recipient -- send a prayer hug. Pray for them, and then send them a note letting them know you have lifted them up to God in prayer.

There is nothing sweeter, nothing safer, nothing more loving, than taking someone to the Lord: for in the presence of God, prayers are heard, hearts are safe, and concerns are met with His unfailing love and grace.

Heavenly Father, I lift up those who will read this post. Bless them with the joy and peace of Your presence. Hug their hearts with Your unfailing love.

Would you be willing to take a moment to send someone a prayer hug?

"I thank my God in all my remembrance of you, always offering prayer with joy in my every prayer for you all." ~ Philippians 1:3-4 (NASB)

Self-Consuming

The enemy loves when we focus on ourselves because inward focus is self-consuming — consuming thoughts, time, and energy. Self-focus is an easy target by the enemy.

Self-focus consumes bite by bite until nothing is left but bitterness, strife, pride, and self-infatuation. Ugh. Self can be so very selfish. When self is torn into pieces there is no peace. We know our needs, because we are a needy lot, and self-needs are so darn needy.

Yes, this Buffaloe needs self-exfoliation. Paul writes, "Rather, clothe yourselves with the Lord Jesus Christ, and do not think about how to gratify the desires of the flesh." ~ Romans 13:14 (NIV)

The cure for self-consuming is moving the focus off self and onto God, for when I am consumed with God and His love, my self-consuming stops.

When I stop looking at myself and my needs and instead look to God and His truth, His word, His love, His blessings, His grace, His mercy, my self finds freedom, new life, healing, love, growth, restoration, hope, peace, and the joy of His perspective.

The only thing I want my self consumed with is loving the Lord my God with all my heart and with all my soul and with all my mind. Because when self is consumed with God, our little selves find beautiful peace and joy!

Heavenly Father, please forgive me for self-consuming, I only want to be consumed by love for You!

Alongside

For months the Lord has been prompting me to watch what He will do. Being the nearsighted woman I am, I've been squinting to see what God is doing in my life. Oh, but then I realized, God is also working in the lives of others. Smack forehead with palm!

It's not just about watching Him work in my life, it's about watching Him work everywhere! God is in the smallest of details inviting us to see His BIG picture.

If we will watch, we'll see Him working in amazing ways. We can pray to have open eyes to focus beyond our near-sighted selves. We can come alongside where God is already working to support, encourage, pray for, and work with others as seed-planters and harvesters for His Kingdom.

Will you pray for open eyes to watch for God?

Where do you see God working? How can you come alongside your brothers and sisters in Christ to help in God's harvest?

Jesus said to his followers, "There are many people to harvest but only a few workers to help harvest them." ~ Matthew 9:37 (NCV)

Surrender

The degree of our love for Christ must be so strong and so focused, that anything or anyone else in our life must seem like hate in relation to the love we have for our Savior. "If anyone comes to Me and does not hate his own father and mother and wife and children and brothers and sisters, yes, and even his own life, he cannot be My disciple." ~ Luke 14:26 (NASB)

What Jesus is asking (commanding) us to do is not negative. Because when we love the Lord with our heart, soul, mind, and strength, we are given God's truth, wisdom, guidance, and joy to freely love others with His truth, wisdom, guidance, and joy. When our love for family, friends, or ideals becomes stronger than the love for Jesus, we risk falling away from God's truth.

For months I fought against the gentle tug to step aside from friendships that had become all-consuming. My health started to suffer, and still I couldn't figure out what was wrong.

A distance and silence with heaven left me crying out. Finally, the answer came, "***You've lost your first love.***" I still didn't understand. Wasn't time with Christian friends part of that love pursuit?

Migraines and stomach problems still didn't clue in this clueless woman. By the time I finally pulled away, the results left friendships in tatters and my heart wounded and weary.

God <u>must</u> be first. Christian friendships are important. Accountability to the body of Christ is important, yet when friendships become more important than God, they have become idols. Loving God must be first.

When loving others more than God, I have nothing more to give. By loving God best, I can give my best to those I love.

There is an old hymn that speaks, "All to Jesus I surrender, all to Him I freely give." When surrendering friendships, some will be gracious, some won't like it, and some won't understand.

Following God means there will be times you won't always align with where others think you should be, or what others think you should do, but following Jesus must be first.

With following God there is always surrender. It's painful, so very painful at times, but without surrender there is no freedom.

Take up your cross and following Jesus is a one road, one-person job. Yes, there will be others along the road to help carry the load, but your cross is your cross, and your following is your path.

Our love has to be God first, because His Love leads us in the true love.

Surrender to Jesus all and you receive His amazing, wonderful, joyful ALL!

Will you surrender all?

Bucket Brigade

Be part of the bucket brigade. Pass on what God has shared with you.

Pass on His good news.

Pass on your bucket of blessings.

Pass on what God shares with you through your actions, words, finances, your daily walk, and your daily life.

Pass on the blessing of being saved by Jesus Christ, by telling others they too can be saved by Jesus Christ.

Pass on The Living Water to those thirsting for truth.

Pass on the God's quenching grace to those in the fire of sin.

Pass on The Bread of Life to starving souls.

Pass on the bucket of blessings that God blesses you with every day.

Pass on the buckets of joy found in the presence of God.

Pass on the bucket of God's love, grace, mercy, healing, and joy.

Until God calls you home be part of the bucket brigade. Pass on God's love to those He has given to love, reach out to those who are hurting. Use your life for His glory and honor. Dive deep in His word and mine the treasure of truths waiting to be discovered. Sing His praises. Point the lost to The One who is The Way – Jesus. He is the one who brings salvation, hope, and healing.

Be part of God's bucket brigade passing on His good news!

Freely you have received, freely give. ~ Matthew 10:8

Praise TNT

Life is a battlefield and it's easy to want to wave the white flag and just sit and moan.

It is so easy to be overwhelmed by all the horrible news, the tragedies, evil, and injustice of this world.

Yet hard days, difficult days, heart-wrenching days, good days, bad days, downright ugly days, are days to praise.

Why praise?

Wesley Duewel writes, "Praise is the Christian's heavy artillery; praise is more effective in spiritual warfare than is an atom bomb in military battle." *

The enemy wants you to think your situation is impossible, but remember with God all things are possible, so praise God.

The enemy wants you to think you've been defeated, remember the devil has already been defeated, so praise God for His victory.

The enemy wants you to do nothing but whine, instead praise God and let His light shine.

The enemy wants you to give up, instead look up and praise God.

When we come to God in praise and thanksgiving, we aren't ignoring our problems, heartaches, or concerns. Praise and thanksgiving rights our thinking, lifts our souls, and lifts our countenance to remember God's MIGHT, POWER, and MAJESTY. His love is unfailing, His might and power are inexhaustible, and the evil forces of this world will fall! God always triumphs.

The last thing the enemy wants you to do is praise, so praise away and let those spiritual bombs fly in the MIGHT, POWER, and MAJESTY of our AWESOME GOD!

"Enter into His gates with thanksgiving, and into His courts with praise. Be thankful to Him and bless His name." ~ Psalm 100:4 (NKJV)

*Wesley L. Duewel, *Touch the World through Prayer*, Michigan: Zondervan, 1986, p 138, 142

Finding Joy and Strength

The more verses I read, study, and dissect; the more I find a common thread – Joy!

Joy is found by spending time with God, obeying Him, thanking Him, reading His word, praising (through word and song), and abiding and dwelling in His presence.

Joy comes through reading, knowing, memorizing scripture. God's word is also called the Sword of the Spirit. God's word is an offensive weapon and if we don't study, read, and memorize scripture, we might as well be twiddling toothpicks at the enemy instead of wielding powerful swords. When Jesus was tempted by the devil, He quoted scripture. Scripture, Bible verses are one of the keys to living a joyful life and walking in freedom.

When we know God's word, we also are given the joy of abiding in Christ, because we know how to live in Christ. Jesus said if we keep His commandments, we will abide in His love, and that His joy would be in us and our joy would be made full. (John 15:10-11) Since in God's presence is fullness of joy, and Jesus is joy, and lives in our hearts and one of the fruits of the Spirit is joy, then joy is always with us, we can rejoice always because joy is in us with us lives in us.

God is The One who brings joy, and Jesus is the one who gives access to The Father. When Jesus is Lord of our lives, joy comes through His grace, mercy, and love. Joy is Jesus, and the joy He gives is the joy we receive when we come to Him.

God's joy is the perfect picture of a perfect, loving relationship. The love God gives is the love we all long for, He is The One who will cuddle next to our hearts when we cuddle up to Him. God is The One who listens to our hearts. God is The One who won't ever misunderstand us, will know exactly what we mean, even when our words are jumbled, confused, a desperate whisper, or merely a groan.

There is an awesome connection when we trust God, enjoy Him, obey Him, abide in Him and His love, and are thankful, for when we do, we are strengthened and infused with His joy.

Joy comes from taking the focus off ourselves, our problems, our wants, our weaknesses, and focusing to enjoy God and His power. As we enjoy God and His amazing blessings, we are strengthened in our inner man (or woman). Joy is beyond circumstances, possessions, or people. Joy is found in the dwelling power of Christ.

In God's presence is fullness of joy and pleasures forever. In His joy we find His strength. God is our strength and shield, and our helper. God's power is with us no matter how weak our flesh.

As we keep God's commands, we abide in His love and in His love, we find His joy (full joy!)

Heavenly Father thank You for Your joy. And thank You for the full joy that comes from Your strength, and the strength that comes from Your joy!

(Psalm 16:11, Nehemiah 8:10, Psalm 28:7, 2 Corinthians 12:9-10, John 15:10-11).

No One Taught Her to Pray

We watched the movie, *Gravity*, with Sandra Bullock. Her character was in a life-threatening situation, and in her fear and anguish she commented that no one taught her how to pray. My heart broke, and I longed to jump into the movie and sit with the character and tell her God was waiting to hear from her. Yes, I know it's only a movie. But I wonder how many people feel that way?

How many people would love to pray but don't feel they know how, or that they have a right, or they aren't cleaned up enough to pray to God?

Oh, please know, you can always pray. Prayer is talking to God. To put it more plainly, prayer is talking to The One who made you, to The One who delights in you and longs for you to have a relationship rooted in His love.

You don't have to know Christian quotes or church phrases to pray. You don't have to chant some mantra; you can talk to God freely and openly. Talk to Him like you would your best friend, to the one who loves you the most, and loves you the best. Because that is God! He loves you best and loves to hear from you.

Talk to God. Pray. God is waiting to hear from you. No concern is too small or too big for our loving God. Nothing you say will shock or surprise Him. No difficulty or situation is beyond God's care.

Pray = communication.

Talk, cry, scream, whimper, or whisper, God is waiting to hear from you.

"I love the Lord, because he listens to my prayers for help. He paid attention to me, so I will call to him for help as long as I live." ~ Psalm 116:1-2 (NCV)

Reporting

One of our favorite restaurants when we lived in Idaho was the Bodacious Pig. They have the best barbecue ever! Without hesitation and without shame, we shared with others about the great food we had found.

When we see a great movie, I love sharing about that movie. What we love, we love to share. So why the hesitation to share about God? As Christians, we don't have to deliver a five-point sermon, we just have to tell others what God has done for us. Tell them about The One you love.

While Jesus walked this earth, the news about Him spread quickly because people shared the news about Jesus. We don't have to have all the answers; all we have to do is share and point them to the One who is the answer.

When Jesus healed a demon-possessed man, Jesus told him "...report to them what great things the Lord has done for you, and how He had mercy on you" (Mark 5:19).

Will you be a reporter? Share the good news and report to others what Jesus has done for you!

Great Expectations

God has really been working on me to fully believe He is all I need and to trust Him. Unfortunately, I'll fret and worry, finally run to Him for help, and thankfully He gently shows His sufficiency. The process keeps being repeated with various situations.

Goodness, you would think I would learn.

I must admit my prayers have been going strong, but my faith has been lacking. Why am I praying yet not believing?

I believe God loves me, I know all things will work to the good, I know He hears when I call, so why have I been mentally running around like a chicken with my head cut off—constantly begging God for help, direction, and guidance?

I finally had an "A-ha!" moment when reading a devotion by Mary Southerland on prayer and faith. She related the story of a small country town in need of rain. The pastor of a church called for a prayer meeting to pray and ask God to fill their desperate need. A crowd gathered, and yet the pastor remarked only one came in faith. He pointed out a small girl who had brought her umbrella.

Yowza, I forgot my faith umbrella!

There is no difficulty, no problem, and no situation God cannot handle. He provides for every need. God is always faithful. What He begins, He perfects, and completes.

I'll keep on praying, but I'm going to live in a state of expectation and bring my faith umbrella, raincoat, and rubber boots!

Let's pray with great expectation!

"Those who wait for the Lord [who expect, look for, and hope in Him] shall change and renew their strength and power; they shall lift their wings and mount up [close to God] as eagles [mount up to the sun]; they shall run and not be weary, they shall walk and not faint or become tired" ~ Isaiah 40:31 (AMP).

"And I am convinced and sure of this very thing, that He Who began a good work in you will continue until the day of Jesus

Christ [right up to the time of His return], developing [that good work] and perfecting and bringing it to full completion in you" ~ Philippians 1:6 (AMP).

Linking Hands

What if our every goal was to promote Christ? What if we would all share what would uplift, encourage, motivate, and draw people to Christ?

Can you imagine what our churches, neighborhoods, work environments, social sites, and our conversations, would be like if we truly lived as one in the unity as Christ desires?

What if we linked hands in spreading the Good News?

Our love would multiply as we loved with the love of Christ.

Our peace would multiply as we shared the peace of God.

Our contentment would multiply as we blessed others with contentment.

Our life would multiply as life is freely given.

Our joy would multiply as we multiplied the joy of the Lord.

Will you link hands in promoting Christ? Where can you link hands to share Christ?

"You too, I urge you, rejoice in the same way and share your joy with me." ~ Philippians 2:18 (NASB)

"Instruct them to do good, to be rich in good works, to be generous and ready to share." ~ 1 Timothy 6:18 (NASB)

Thanksgiving, More Than A Holiday

Thanksgiving is more than a holiday. The word Thanksgiving brings smiles to many and sadness to others. It's a word associated with a holiday with images of Norman Rockwell paintings of family sharing food and laughter around a bountiful table. However, the images for most aren't real. Families are scattered by distance, painful memories, sin, death, and heartache, and holidays only make many hearts depressed and lonely.

Thanksgiving is a word that means so much more. Thanksgiving is a thankful heart for the grace and mercy of Jesus Christ.

Jesus is the Savior who comes to live in hearts that have felt distanced, have painful memories, sin, death of dreams and loved ones, and heartache. Jesus comes inside hearts and lives, and restores, and redeems, and never leaves, and always loves.

When we are thankful, thanksgiving replaces emotions with reality, the reality of a life eternal, rising the soul above the painfulness and frailty of life. Thanksgiving is more than a holiday; thanksgiving is a lifestyle.

The more we style our life on thankfulness, the more our eyes are open to see God's blessings, provision, faithfulness, and love.

If your life is good, be thankful.

If your life is hard and miserable, thank God He will help you through and never leave you.

There is always something for which to be thankful.

Please know, never forget, even during times of loneliness our tender God is there to hold you close, sit quietly with you, and love you through the sadness of any day. You are never alone, never alone.

Be thankful, for you are eternally and unfailingly loved!

In Your unfailing love You will lead the people You have redeemed. In Your strength You will guide them to Your holy dwelling. Let them give thanks to the Lord for his unfailing love

and his wonderful deeds for mankind. I trust in your unfailing love;
my heart rejoices in your salvation. How priceless is your unfailing
love, O God! People take refuge in the shadow of your wings
(Exodus 15:13, Psalm 107:8, Psalm 13:5, Psalm 36:7)

Yielded

I find it interesting to contemplate the many ways Christian life seems opposite the world. Society wants to hoard, while God says to give. Jesus came from glory to walk the dusty roads to show us the way off the dusty roads to live in glory.

God's ways are higher, better, and more amazing than we can imagine.

In the yielding, laying down of self, we find complete freedom in Christ. The yielded vessel receives the blessing. We die to self to be filled with Jesus. We lay down ourselves to be picked up by Him. We lay down what we think we need to receive all we need in Christ. We lay down our control to be totally controlled by Christ.

Give Jesus your all and you'll receive more of His joy, more of His peace, and more of Him.

What areas do you need to yield to God to live in His freedom?

"Give, and it will be given to you. They will pour into your lap a good measure—pressed down, shaken together, and running over. For by your standard of measure it will be measured to you in return." ~ Luke 6:38 (NASB)

Chiseled

Have you ever seen the statues by the great masters? Can you imagine the time each masterpiece would have taken?

Visualize the care of each strike of the chisel, the amazing detail carved from a rough stone, the delicate smoothing, and the precision of every move until the statue stands in perfection.

What if the stone objected to the strike of the chisel? What if it had refused to allow the work done?

How many of us are unfinished masterpieces because we refuse the work the Master wants to complete?

"We may wish, indeed, that we were of so little account to God that He left us alone to follow our natural impulses — that He would give over trying to train us into something so unlike our natural selves: .... we are asking not for more love, but for less... To ask that God's love should be content with us as we are is to ask that God should cease to be God: because He is what He is, His love must, in the nature of things, be impeded and repelled by certain stains in our present character and because He already loves us He must labor to make us loveable." ~ C. S. Lewis*

Will you allow the Master's Hand to complete His work in you?

Heavenly Father I'm not fond of the chiseling, but I do love Your finished products. Thank You for Your loving touch that continues working on me so I may be all You desire.

"And I am convinced and sure of this very thing, that He Who began a good work in you will continue until the day of Jesus Christ [right up to the time of His return], developing [that good work] and perfecting and bringing it to full completion in you." ~ Philippians 1:6 (AMP)

*C.S. Lewis, *The Problem of Pain*, (New York, NY: MacMillan Publishing Co. Inc., 1962), pp. 42,48.

Diving to the Depths

Paul, Peter, James, and others mentioned in the Bible, didn't just know God, they longed to know the mighty depths of God. Depths that transcend fear of death, beatings, stoning, and living without earthly comfort.

Surface swimmers may think they are playing with a "safe" Christianity that allows them to swim in the world and still have a toe in salvation. But only a toe isn't what saves. Christ tells us to die to self, to abide in Him through obedience and following His commandments.

Cheap talk about Christianity doesn't result in lifesaving, life-changing Christianity.

Deep calls to deep, and the deep truths of God's love, holiness, power, grace, and mercy call to each one of us. For there is no deep too deep for the love of Christ.

The love of Christ is deep, wide, beautiful, and soul filling. Like Paul I pray that "Christ may dwell in your hearts through faith; that you, being rooted and grounded in love, may be able to comprehend with all the saints what is the width and length and depth and height—to know the love of Christ which passes knowledge; that you may be filled with all the fullness of God." ~ Ephesians 3:17-19 (NKJV)

Deep wisdom is available through God for every need, and His wisdom is steeped in the depth of God's love.

Don't just skim the surface, dive to the depths of God's word, His truth, His love, and His majesty.

Live deep in the loving heart of God to point others to the depth of His love.

"Oh, the depth of the riches both the wisdom and knowledge of God! How unsearchable are His judgments and His ways past finding out!" ~ Romans 11:33 (NKJV)

"For I am persuaded that neither death nor life, nor angels nor principalities nor powers, nor things present nor things to come, nor height nor depth, nor any other created thing, shall be able to

separate us from the love of God which is in Christ Jesus our Lord."
~ Romans 8:38-39 (NKJV)

"Eye has not seen, nor ear heard, nor have entered into the heart of man the things which God has prepared for those who love Him.' But God has revealed them to us through His Spirit. For the Spirit searches all things, yes, the deep things of God." ~ 1 Corinthians 2:9-10 (NKJV)

Throne Room Prayers

I prayed on the phone with a precious friend, and my prayers were good, fine, and acceptable. But when my friend prayed, I was driven to my knees, my head bowed in adoration and worship. I'm still humbled by her prayer, and still feel the presence of the Lord in the room as she prayed.

My prayers were good, but her prayers led us into The Throne Room of our Mighty King.

I've been in The Throne Room with many prayers. I've sat at God's feet and marveled. Yet my heart breaks as I realize not every prayer is a Throne Room prayer. At times, in the familiar walk with God, I've forgotten His holiness.

I wonder if at times our prayers don't reach higher than the ceiling because we want His blessings without obeying Him. We want His goodness, without living holy lives. We want His ear without having listening ears. We want physical well-being without spiritual wellness.

We want His Living Water yet refuse to drink. We want The Bread of Life, without dining with The Bread of Life. And we wonder why we aren't in the Throne Room of His Presence.

Will you come to God's throne room in prayer?

"As He who called you is holy, you also be holy in all your conduct, because it is written, 'Be holy, for I am holy.' Call to Me, and I will answer you, and show you great and mighty things, which you do not know. And you will seek Me and find Me, when you search for Me with all your heart." ~ 1 Peter 1:15-16 (NKJV), Jeremiah 33:3 (NKJV), Jeremiah 29:13 (NKJV)

Flaming

I'm at that age. Yes, "that" age. **Hot** flashes. Argh! One minute I'm freezing and the next I'm flaming.

Hot flashes seem to be worse at night. I'll be nice and snug in my blankets, when all of the sudden my internal regulator switches to super-flame. Goodness, I've become the human firefly.

The only thing I want burning is my zeal for Christ. I don't want to be cold or lukewarm. I want to flame for God.

I love Luke 24:32 where the men encounter the risen Lord and "They asked each other, 'Were not our hearts burning within us while he talked with us on the road and opened the Scriptures to us?'"

The wonderful thing is, we don't have to be a certain age or gender to experience a burning heart. Encounters with Christ, His word, His truth, and His love, change us. Spending time in His presence fans the flame.

Heavenly Father, make my heart burn with passion for You, Your word, and Your presence. Let me flame always for You!

As a Christian

Truth for you as a Christian...

As a Christian, I have Christ within me. I have His power. I can do all things through Christ who strengthens me. I am never powerless with the power of Christ. Even when I am weak, He is strong. His strength is within me. I have HIS POWER. And nothing is impossible for God!

As a Christian, I have wisdom for every problem and situation, for God gives wisdom generously without reproach to all who ask.

As a Christian, I'll know the way, because Jesus is The Way.

As a Christian, I have the love of the Father living inside me. I can love even when my love is waning. I can love the unlovely because I am loved by the loveliest even when I was the most unlovable.

As a Christian, I have hope, even when I can't see a reason to hope, God's hope is eternal and thus I can hope. He is hope so I am never hopeless.

As a Christian I am given the joy of Jesus. Even when I don't feel joy, Jesus lives in my heart, so His joy is within my heart. As a Christian I'll get myself out of the way with all the emotions (and lack of emotions) and will allow Jesus' joy to joyfully bubble up and out of me.

As a Christian I have God's truth. The world is so confusing sometimes, life is so confusing, but God's truth stands firm. He will guide me in His truth.

As a Christian I am graced with eternal life. Even when my brain and body feel lifeless, His life courses through my veins to give His abundant life.

As a Christian I have the peace from The Prince of peace. And His peace passes the world's understanding.

As a Christian, I have the blessing of God's comfort through His Holy Spirit.

As a Christian, I have God's presence. I need never be lonely. I'm never without a friend. A true friend. A loving friend. And am never without a home for my heart.

Embrace the truth of who you are in Christ!

Doing Business

Jesus said, "A nobleman went to a distant country to receive a kingdom for himself, and then return. And he called ten of his slaves, and gave them ten minas and said to them, 'Do business with this until I come back.'"

Two servants invested the money, and one did nothing with what he was given. When the nobleman "returned, having received the kingdom, he ordered these servants to whom he had given the money to be called to him, that he might know what they had gained by doing business" (Luke 19:12-27).

The two servants who invested and multiplied what they were given, were blessed. The one who did nothing with the money, lost what little he had.

I read these verses and wondered are we being faithful to "do business" with what God has gifted us?

Our talents and giftings may look small in the world's eyes, but in the Kingdom of God they are huge.

Every encouraging word, every prayer prayed, every hand that reaches out to comfort and help in the name of Jesus are investments in God's Kingdom. Caring for your family, shining God's light in the dark world all are valuable. Every day you can do business for God's kingdom.

What has God invested in you? Are you faithful to use your talents and blessings to multiply those talents and blessings for His kingdom?

Until the Lord returns, or we are called home, let's make sure to be about our Father's business.

Heavenly Father, help me to be faithful and be about your business, so one day I may hear... "Well done, good and faithful servant. Enter into the joy of your master" (Matthew 25:21).

Wrapped Up

When we lived in Texas, we had a beautiful azalea bush in our backyard. Planted under a small tree for shade, we watered and tenderly cared for it, yet the azalea refused to grow.

The rapid demise didn't make sense until we pulled it from the ground and discovered the roots had never left the root ball. The plant had been totally wrapped up in itself.

Sometimes it hurts to break out of our own little root balls, and it can be painful trying to dig through rocky soil, stretching out as we grow and mature.

Fortunately, God loves us too much to leave us wrapped up in ourselves. His goal is to conform us to the image of His Son. God is our Creator and knows our potential. When He beckons us to step outside of our comfort zones, He has good things planned for our growth and the growth of His kingdom.

I don't want to be so wrapped up in myself that I miss God's amazing blessings.

Heavenly Father, please forgive me when I don't want to leave my comfort zone. Please help me to remember Your plans are always best and often they are found in the place of the most growth. Grow me in You so I may grow for You.

"Grow in the grace and knowledge of our Lord and Savior Jesus Christ." ~ 2 Peter 3:18

Like Children

Jesus said we are to come to Him as little children (Matthew 18:3). How do those of us who are older, remember how to be a child?

Age is relative. Regardless of our age, we are mere children to an eternal God. We can come as children even when we don't understand how to come, knowing He will guide and lead us. We can come into His presence with confidence knowing He is a loving Father.

Jesus beckons us to come as children, to come unhindered by our own agendas, thoughts, and the tainted worldview. The invitation is the invitation to live in freedom to love and be loved.

Yet how do we live as children and live in the freedom of innocence when the world has tainted, darkened, and stained? The good news is, even if our innocence was stolen by others, we have the return of innocence in the pure, clean, clear truth of God and His love. His restoration is complete.

We have freedom to obey as children, because we can throw off our untrusting thoughts and return to the innocence of childhood. God promises to provide, so like little children, we trust and obey.

Come to God as His child. You are loved by your Heavenly Father. Come unhindered, come in freedom, come to His healing, come joyfully to His perfect love.

"But as many as received Him, to them He gave the right to become children of God, to those who believe in His name." ~ John 1:12 (NKJV)

"See what great love the Father has lavished on us, that we should be called children of God! And that is what we are!" ~ 1 John 3:1 (NIV)

Can or Called?

I'm a "can do" kind of woman. I have knowledge, some strength and power, and the means and capacity to do and accomplish many things. I can keep incredibly busy with family, friends, writing, and social interactions. However, having a "can do" attitude isn't necessarily a calling.

The Greek definition of "called" is a calling, an invitation, an invitation to a feast, a divine invitation to embrace the salvation of God.

When we take the time to assess our calling as opposed to what we can accomplish on our own, we find the power, strength, motivation, and supply of God.

If I change my thoughts from "doing what I can do" to "doing what I've been called to do", that is where supernatural empowering comes, for nothing is impossible with God and His power can do all things.

Our callings are so much bigger than anything we can do on our own. What we are called to do is amazing.

Read through this list of just some of the things God will supply you for your calling.

As Christians, we are gifted to be irrevocably called. "God's gifts and his call are irrevocable." ~ Romans 11:29 (NIV)

We are called to hope. "There is one body and one Spirit, just as you were called to one hope when you were called." ~ Ephesians 4:4 (NIV)

We are called to be free. "You, my brothers and sisters, were called to be free. But do not use your freedom to indulge the flesh; rather, serve one another humbly in love." ~ Galatians 5:13 (NIV)

We are called to power and strength through Christ. "To those whom God has called, both Jews and Greeks, Christ the power of God and the wisdom of God for the foolishness of God is wiser than human wisdom, and the weakness of God is stronger than human strength." ~ 1 Corinthians 1:24-25 (NIV)

We are called to fellowship with Jesus Christ. "God is faithful, through whom you were called into fellowship with His Son, Jesus Christ our Lord." ~ 1 Corinthians 1:9 (NASB)

We are called for justification and glory. "Whom He predestined, He also called; and these whom He called, He also justified; and these whom He justified, He also glorified. He called you to this through our gospel, that you might share in the glory of our Lord Jesus Christ." ~ Romans 8:30 (NASB), 2 Thessalonians 2:14 (NIV)

We are called to fight the good fight. "Fight the good fight of the faith. Take hold of the eternal life to which you were called when you made your good confession in the presence of many witnesses." ~ 1 Timothy 6:12 (NIV)

We are called to belong. "Called to belong to Jesus Christ." ~ Romans 1:6

We are called to be holy. "But just as he who called you is holy, so be holy in all you do." ~ 1 Peter 1:15 (NIV)

We are called not because of works but according to God's purpose and grace. "He saved us and called us with a holy calling, not according to our works, but according to His own purpose and grace which was given to us in Christ Jesus before time began." ~ 2 Timothy 1:9 (NKJV)

We are called to press on for a heavenly prize. "I press on toward the goal to win the prize for which God has called me heavenward in Christ Jesus." ~ Philippians 3:14 (NIV)

We are called to an eternal inheritance and freedom. "Christ is the mediator of a new covenant, that those who are called may receive the promised eternal inheritance—now that he has died as a ransom to set them free from the sins committed under the first covenant." ~ Hebrews 9:15 (NIV)

We are called to peace and thankfulness to allow the peace of Christ to rule in our hearts and to be thankful (Colossians 3:15).

We are called out of darkness into light. "But you are a chosen people, a royal priesthood, a holy nation, God's special possession, that you may declare the praises of him who called you out of darkness into his wonderful light." ~ 1 Peter 2:9 (NIV)

We are called to endure. "But how is it to your credit if you receive a beating for doing wrong and endure it? But if you suffer for doing good and you endure it, this is commendable before God. To this you were called, because Christ suffered for you, leaving you an example, that you should follow in his steps." ~ 1 Peter 2:20-21 (NIV)

We are called to bless. "Do not repay evil with evil or insult with insult. On the contrary, repay evil with blessing, because to this you were called so that you may inherit a blessing." ~ 1 Peter 3:9 (NIV)

We are called to restoration, strength, firmness, and steadfastness. "And the God of all grace, who called you to his eternal glory in Christ, after you have suffered a little while, will himself restore you and make you strong, firm and steadfast." ~ 1 Peter 5:10 (NIV)

We are called and given everything needed. "His divine power has given us everything we need for a godly life through our knowledge of him who called us by his own glory and goodness." ~ 2 Peter 1:3 (NIV)

We are called to be loved and kept. "To those who have been called, who are loved in God the Father and kept for Jesus Christ." ~ Jude 1:1 (NIV)

We are called to be friends. "I no longer call you servants, because a servant does not know his master's business. Instead, I have called you friends, for everything that I learned from my Father I have made known to you." ~ John 15:15 (NIV)

We are called in love to be God's child. "See what great love the Father has lavished on us, that we should be called children of God! And that is what we are!" ~ 1 John 3:1 (NIV)

So, my dear friends, "I urge you to live a life worthy of the calling you have received." ~ Ephesians 4:1 (NIV)

I'll let Paul finish this section. "I pray that the eyes of your heart may be enlightened, so that you will know what is the hope of His calling, what are the riches of the glory of His inheritance in the saints, and what is the surpassing greatness of His power toward us who believe. These are in accordance with the working of the strength of His might which He brought about in Christ, when He raised Him from the dead and seated Him at His right hand in the heavenly places, far above all rule and authority and power and dominion, and every name that is named, not only in this age but also in the one to come." ~ Ephesians 1:18-21 (NASB)

Enjoy your God-given callings!

Supernatural International Guard

Wherever you are, whatever you do, if you are a follower of Jesus Christ, you are stationed throughout the world in His supernatural international guard. You are to God's hands and feet, His voice of truth to spread His love and hope. You've been commissioned to go, tell, and make disciples.

A hurting world waits, when life's tragedies come, be there with a shoulder to lean on, a helping hand, prayers, encouragement, and love.

Go. Tell. Make Disciples.

Go – Go inside your own home, in your neighborhood, in your state, in your country, in a foreign land, go wherever Christ leads you.

Tell – Tell others how Christ has changed your life. Tell them of the hope that they also can find in Christ. Tell them of the grace and mercy through Jesus Christ.

Make Disciples – Share God's Word, share God's truth, share Christ. Show them God's love. A hurting world waits, and you are needed to help spread God's love and His good news!

Where can you go and who can you tell about our awesome God and Savior, Jesus Christ?

"Therefore, go and make disciples of all the nations, baptizing them in the name of the Father and the Son and the Holy Spirit." ~ Matthew 28:19 (NLT)

Sharing Seeds

Our bird feeder contains several tasty options for our feathered friends. Finches, sparrows, and dove are our most common visitors. The finches at first puzzled me, and I thought they were terribly messy. While they ate, seeds would fly right and left. Then I watched closer, the finches used their beaks to sweep side to side sending the seeds scattering to the ground.

Larger birds are too big to fit on the edge of our feeder, and these tiny finches share in the bounty. Quail, robins, red-winged blackbirds, other finches, and sparrows gather underneath to reap the harvest.

I think I'd like to mimic a finch and take the goodness of God's word to share with a hungry world.

There's plenty of room on the perch. Want to join me in scattering seeds?

Where can you share the seeds of God's word?

"I do everything to spread the Good News and share in its blessings." ~ 1 Corinthians 9:23 (NLT)

Stop the Phooey!

If we look for success, confirmation, and legitimization through the world's eyes instead of the uniqueness of God's eyes we will always struggle.

We hear others tell us we're only successful if...

We're popular.

We're in upper management.

Our blog, Facebook page, or Twitter feed has xxxx followers.

We do things like the other successful people.

We dress like they do, think like they do, become like they are.

We're in "this" organization, or "that" neighborhood, or you have "this", or you did "that" ...

Phooey!

If worth is based on the world's ideals, we will always be lacking.

No matter who you are, there will always be someone else more popular. Someone in the future, someone in the past. Someone else will always take your place.

The one who is the most powerful, most beautiful, most successful, will always be replaced by someone else more powerful, more beautiful, or more successful. The target is always moving and always subjective.

If you are looking to be legitimized by man, you will always be deficient.

If you are trying to be the perfect employee, perfect wife, perfect husband, perfect athlete, perfect author/singer/speaker, perfect parent, perfect anything ... **Stop!**

We're so busy listening to people we don't listen to God's truth. We are so busy looking at others giftings, possessions, and blessings, we don't notice what God has given us.

If we all try to be like everyone else, there will be no individuality, there would be no one who stands out from the crowd, and no one available for God to use in ways beyond man's thinking.

Christians aren't to be conformed to the world's image; we are to be transformed to the image of Christ.

You are created unique for unique purposes; don't miss the beauty of who you are created to be.

Allow God to work in you and through you. Allow His creativity to flow through your perfectly-heaven-created veins to be used in perfectly unique and amazing ways.

Don't strive for self-worth, our job is to surrender. Freely surrender so the Master Artist can fully transform us into His perfect Son – Jesus Christ.

Heavenly Father, I'm so tired of worrying about what others think. I'm so tired of looking for self-worth in the selfish world. Oh Father, I submit and surrender to You. Mold me and make me in the image of Your Son, Jesus Christ. Help me to fully embrace You so that I may fully embrace who You created me to be. Help me to keep my focus on You so that I see my worth solely through Your eyes, because in You and through You I find my perfect worth.

Burning Out the Hesitation

At times I'm hesitant to write, stymied and wondering if my motives are pure. Some hesitation comes from the enemy placing doubts and questioning why I should I even try.

However, if no one visited my blogs, if my books never sold, would I keep writing to tell others about Him? If everything went away – if I lost everything, would I still love God?

Yes!

As Jeremiah wrote, "But if I say, 'I will not remember Him or speak anymore in His name,' then in my heart it becomes like a burning fire shut up in my bones; and I am weary of holding it in, and I cannot endure it." ~ Jeremiah 20:9 (NASB)

When the hesitation comes, I pray the Lord will kindle afresh and fan into flame the desire to continue to speak and write for Him. Until my final breath and as long as my fingers can type, as long as I can speak, I'll keep sharing about God's amazing, wonderful, incredible, awesome grace, mercy, and love.

To a world living in darkness, how can I not share the light?

To a world hurting and in pain, how can I not share the news of the One who heals, restores, and renews?

To a world so desperately seeking for love and fulfillment, how can I not share the love of God – the true source of unending joy and contentment?

To you, those who are kind enough to visit my social sites and read my books, thank you. Thank you for joining me on this journey.

Are you hesitant to share with others? Is a fire burning in your soul to tell a friend, family member, co-worker about Christ?

Don't let anything stop you from sharing Christ with a world that so needs Christ.

Would you be willing to pray this prayer with me?

Heavenly Father, burn out any hesitation in me that stands in the way of Your perfect will. Fan into flame the fires You have placed in my soul. Let my light always shine bright for You.

Free Flying

God wants to talk with every single one of us (that includes you!). It's amazing to think the God of the universe wants to spend time with us, but He does.

Our communication with God is never confined. We are free to talk with Him at all times of the day or night, and His access is unlimited. God is not restricted to a landline phone or even a cell phone with limited coverage. You don't have to worry if a cell tower is close by, or your battery is charged. God is available 24/7.

Swimming isn't my sport, because if I'm not hot flashing the water is never warm enough. My only method of treading water is the dogpaddle, and the older I get the less appealing it is to reveal any skin to the sun or the public.

Years ago, I stood in a neighborhood pool teaming with squealing, swimming, floating children, with the sound registering on a high decibel level. Although the location seemed less than ideal, for several hours in the midst of the craziness, my soul flew into God's presence, and I enjoyed His company.

Our souls need to fly, because our daily situations can be so confining. We need to plug into God's power source to have strength for the day. We need to know someone wants to listen no matter how long we want to talk or what we need to discuss, and God is always available.

One of my favorite memories is sitting on a large boulder in the middle of a crystal-clear river in the Idaho mountains where I spent time talking with God, singing praise songs, and enjoying His beautiful creation.

Even during times of illness when I could do absolutely nothing but be still, my soul could fly into God's presence.

Do you feel confined by your circumstance? In the noise, in the quiet, our souls can always fly free to commune with God.

"The eyes of the Lord are on the righteous, and His ears are open to their cry." ~ Psalm 34:15 (NKJV)

One Another

I did a search for the phrase, "one another" and found some sweet connections.

Love one another.
Be devoted to one another.
Live in harmony with one another.
Stop passing judgment on one another.
Accept one another.
Avoid divisions among one another.
Serve one another in love.
Be patient with one another.
Be kind and compassionate to one another.
Forgiving one another.
Speak to one another with psalms, hymns, and spiritual songs.
Submit to one another.
Forgive one another as Christ forgave you.
Teach and admonish one another.
Encourage one another.
Spur one another on toward love and good deeds.
Meet with one another.
Do not slander one another.
Love one another deeply.
Live in harmony with one another.
Be sympathetic with one another.
Be compassionate and humble with one another.
Offer hospitality with one another.
Clothe yourselves with humility toward one another.
Believe in the name of his Son, Jesus Christ, and love one another as He commanded us.
If we walk in the light, as He is in the light, we have fellowship with one another.
Let us love one another, for love comes from God. Since God so loved us, we also ought to love one another. If we love one another, God lives in us, and his love is made complete in us.

Heavenly Father, thank You we are never alone on this journey. Help me to always be aware of the "one anothers" in my path. Help me to love, cherish, and speak to them of Your love that died so that we may forever live complete and unified in You.

(John 13:34-35, Romans 12:10, 12: 16, 13:8, 14:13, 15:7, 1 Corinthians 1:10, Galatians 5:13, Ephesians 4:2, 4:32, 5:19, 5:21, Colossians 3:13, 3:16, 1 Thessalonians 5:11, Hebrews 3:13, 10:24-25, James 4:11, 1 Peter 1:22, 3:8, 4:9, 5:5, 1 John 1:7, 3:11, 3:23, 4:7, 4:11-12).

I'm Telling, Will You?

Tell others about God.

Tell them how God saved you.

Tell them what God has done for you.

Tell what God has done for others.

Tell of God's amazing love.

Tell of God's wonderful grace.

Tell of God's bountiful mercy.

Tell your children, friends, family, those you know, and those you meet, about God.

Even "the heavens are telling of the glory of God; and their expanse is declaring the work of His hands." ~ Psalm 19:1 (NASB)

Will you tell?

"I will give thanks to the LORD with all my heart; I will tell of all Your wonders. Come and hear, all who fear God, and I will tell of what He has done for my soul. My mouth shall tell of Your righteousness and of Your salvation all day long; for I do not know the sum of them. The nearness of God is my good; I have made the Lord GOD my refuge, that I may tell of all Your works.

"Tell to the generations to come the praises of the LORD, and His strength and His wondrous works that He has done. That the generation to come might know, even the children yet to be born, that they may arise and tell them to their children.

"So, we Your people and the sheep of Your pasture will give thanks to You forever; to all generations we will tell of Your praise.

"Tell of His glory among the nations, His wonderful deeds among all the peoples.

"Men shall speak of the power of Your awesome acts, And I will tell of Your greatness. But we ourselves cannot help telling what we have seen and heard." ~ Psalm 9:1, Psalm 66:16, Psalm 71:15, Psalm 73:28, Psalm 78:4, Psalm 78:6, Psalm 79:13, Psalm 96:3, Psalm 145:6 (NASB), Acts 4:20 (AMP)

Who can you tell of the wonderful love of God?

Encourage, Please

The definition of encouragement is the act of giving courage, or confidence of success; incitement to action or to practice; incentive.

We all need encouragement. Life is hard and discouraging. We need courage to continue, we need confidence to continue, we need an incentive to continue.

Encourage yourself with God's truth, because the encouragement found in God's word gives the courage, confidence, and the eternal incentive to continue.

God gives power, strength to the weary, never forsakes, never fails, and loves with an unfailing love. His salvation is an eternal blessing, and we are never without hope.

Encourage others, for in the encouragement of others we receive blessings, courage, confidence, and reminders we are in this world together.

The encouragement of others reminds us that we are needed, we are wanted, and with the love of our Heavenly Father we can make a positive impact in this world that so needs encouragement.

Let's encourage, admonish, exhort, edify, strengthen, and build up one another!

May I encourage you to encourage others?

"Therefore encourage (admonish, exhort) one another and edify (strengthen and build up) one another, just as you are doing."
~ 1 Thessalonians 5:11 (AMP)

Silent Invaders

The Honey Mushroom is a fungus that moves silently through the soil coming up through roots then slowly starving and eventually killing trees. One specific honey-fungus covers over 2.4 square mile acres in Oregon and is thought to be the largest living organism in the world.

Silent invaders also infiltrate the church. Beware of those who may look good, perhaps even have a pretty title, yet are busy gossiping, spreading lies, or altering the truth of the Bible to starve outgrowth, hinder, or kill the body of Christ. Be careful of the wolves in sheep clothing. Be careful and be wise.

"Beware of the false prophets, who come to you in sheep's clothing, but inwardly are ravenous wolves." ~ Matthew 7:15 (NASB)

Let's make sure we nourish our Christian brothers and sisters. Encourage and pray for your siblings-in-Christ. Be careful to never hinder God's Spirit from working in your life or the lives of others.

Let's move through the soil of this earth to bring the Good News to those around us and to the lost. Counter the silent invaders with God's truth and God's love.

Move in God's love and let God's love move in you and through you!

"Therefore, if there is any encouragement in Christ, if there is any consolation of love, if there is any fellowship of the Spirit, if any affection and compassion, make my joy complete by being of the same mind, maintaining the same love, united in spirit, intent on one purpose. Let all that you do be done in love" ~ Philippians 2:1-2, 1 Corinthians 16:14 (NASB).

Prayer for Protection

Heavenly Father,

Protect our eyes to be focused on You so we may see You and the wonderful things You do each and every day.

Protect our feet so they may walk with You and go where You want them to go.

Protect our hands so they may be of use for You.

Protect our minds so they may know and meditate on Your truth.

Protect our mouths so they may only speak what is pleasing to You.

Protect our ears so they may be sensitive to always hear Your voice, direction, and guidance.

Protect our thoughts to be centered on You and Your Word.

Protect us Lord, that we may be used for Your glory.

Protect our hearts to beat in tune with the joy of You.

Let all who take refuge in You rejoice; let them ever sing for joy, and spread Your protection over them, that those who love Your name may be joyful in You. ~ Psalm 5:11

About the Author

Lisa Buffaloe is a happily married mom, author, and speaker. When she's not writing, she enjoys working in her yard, exploring God's beautiful nature, and taking long walks with her sweet husband.

Lisa loves sharing God's unending love and that through Him we find healing, restoration, renewal, and joy.

Visit the author at https://lisabuffaloe.com.

Books by Lisa Buffaloe
(Updated July 2023)

Fiction

The Masterpiece Beneath

Nadia's Hope (Hope and Grace Series, Book 1)

Prodigal Nights (Hope and Grace Series, Book 2)

Writing Her Heart (Hope and Grace Series, Book 3)

The Discovery Chapter (Hope and Grace Series, Book 4)

Open Lens (Hope and Grace Series, Book 5)

The Fortune

Grace for the Char-Baked

Non-Fiction

Float by Faith

Heart and Soul Medication

Time with The Timeless One

The Forgotten Resting Place

Present in His Presence

We Were Meant for Paradise

One Lit Step: Devotions for your journey

The Unnamed Devotional

Flying on His Wings

Unfailing Treasures

No Wound Too Deep for The Deep Love of Christ

Living Joyfully Free Devotional, (Volume 1)

Living Joyfully Free Devotional, (Volume 2)

Thank you for reading,

The Unnamed Devotional

Lisa Buffaloe